POLITICS AND THE STATE

POLITICS AND THE STATE
The Catholic View

by Thomas Molnar

FRANCISCAN HERALD PRESS
1434 WEST 51st STREET ● CHICAGO, 60609

Copyright © 1980
FRANCISCAN HERALD PRESS
Chicago, Illinois

Library of Congress Cataloging in Publication Data

Molnar, Thomas Steven.
  Politics and the state, the Catholic view.

  Includes bibliographical references
  1. Christianity and politics. 2. Church and state
—Catholic Church. 3. Church and state—United States.
4. Sociology, Christian (Catholic) 5. United States—
Church history. 6. Political science—History.
I. Title.
BR115.P7M553   261.7   80-10748
ISBN 0-8199-0799-5

Published with Ecclesiastical Permission

MADE IN THE UNITED STATES OF AMERICA

Table of Contents

To the memory of my mother

Preface

Simple common sense dictates that political theory should cover, and deal with, the salient points of political practice, and that, in turn, the latter should be enlightened by theory. Otherwise, events, decisions, and changes in the vast political realm risk floating in a vacuum where reasoning (even about the irrational), judgment, and principles are absent, and the citizen remains blind to the forces which shape his destiny. In this respect, the specific character of America in the second half of this century is the timidity with which its citizens regard political theory, unless political practice in its routine aspects gives it the green light. American pragmatism consists in granting primacy to the so-called practical, and inasmuch as theory would chart new ways of looking at things, people shun it because they see in any new or unaccustomed theory an implicit critique of the "way things are" and indeed, of the American way of life itself.

The consequence of this attitude is that only three political theories are today considered respectable (we are not speaking here of sociological, psycho-social, economic or anthropological theories), and that a fourth one is tolerated as marginal, almost "un-American." The fourth one, to begin with that, is Marxist theory which, in spite of the popularity of its advocates in some academic circles, has not entered the mainstream of American political thought. The three main political schools are then the following: the theory for which the *Federalist Papers* constitute the central frame of reference, a document that conservatives and liberals alike may claim as theirs. Hence, the endless efforts to interpret and scrutinize the "Federalist", itself a somewhat ambiguous document the authors of which belonged to divergent schools of thought. The second theory that has spectacularly moved into the authorized area of debate is associated with the name of *Leo Strauss,* whose influence has now reached the third generation of "Straussians." The third theory, suffering at the start from certain handicaps, then become increasingly respectable, is the one elaborated by *Eric Voegelin*

While the liberal academicians have many theories to choose from and to identify themselves with—not because they are politically imaginative but because they are freer to mix politics with other disciplines—their conservative colleagues have, for all intents and purposes, locked themselves up in a compound delimited by the Federalist Papers, the Straussian and the Voegelinian schools. One may argue that these three schools present them—and American political theorizing in general—with a sufficiently rich material for the evaluation of political reality, yet such an argument would be only partly true. At first sight, the Federalist Papers represent British-American political thought at its most mature, and the Voegelinian and Straussian schools bring to the American scene the thought of Europe, rooted in the classical, mostly Greek, tradition. Fact is, however, that the combined image that these three modes of thought present, still leaves out some essential ingredients of western political teaching and experience. These ingredients are uniquely contained in the Catholic concept of politics and the State.

The three schools we mentioned cannot be indicted for what each teaches, but rather for what none of them includes in its discourse. In this respect, they commit more or less the same error as those textbooks—of literature, political thought, history of art, the evolution of science—in which the last mentioned premodern significant figure or achievement is still part of the ancient world of Greece and Rome, and the next significant figure or achievement belongs to the Renaissance; in between there are the "dark ages", unworthy of mention, let alone discussion. The speculative roots of the Federalist Papers are admittedly in the Roman republic (as well as in English history), and this is understandable in view of the period of writing, the rationalistic age of Enlightenment. But Strauss and Voegelin also narrowed their universe of discourse: the world-picture of Strauss is bordered by Plato and Maimonides, that of Voegelin by Plato and Aristotle. Two consequences follow from this manner of viewing things: one is that both thinkers locate the *acme* of western political development *in the past,* more precisely in the Greek past. From then on, and in comparison to which, everything is regarded by these authors as decline, degradation, loss of object. The other consequence is that both thinkers put too heavy an emphasis on the theoretical side of politics, as if the latter consisted only of the speculations of periodically emerging great minds, with negligible areas in between.

No matter how admirable such great minds were, they were compelled to *theorize* about the concrete, not to *deal* with it. The result was a limitation to theoretical constructs, such as the "well-ordered polis", the "just republic", the "utopia", or the "classless society". Voegelin is primarily interested in the symbolization of community experience which finds expression in myth or in philosophy; Strauss focuses on natural law illumined by the ethical command as it is taught by the insights of the prophet or the prophet-like philosopher.

In contrast, the Catholic tradition is one of theory *and* practice, intermingled, because theory developed at the contact of historical events in which the Church took a most active part, either as victim of persecution, as a shaper of society, or as a holder of authority. But, even more important, this continuity of involvement with concrete political realities was paralleled by the continuity of a solidly held concept of man, society, and the nature of politics, an unchanging concept rooted in revelation and in the structure of human nature. In turn, this concept has been tested in the fire of changing historical configurations, in pagan Rome, and Constantinian period, the Germanic kingdoms, the feudal age, romanticism, democracy, socialism, and beyond. It is tested in our own time, in the most diverse ways and places.

The wisdom and experience thus accumulated are unmatched by any, temporarily fashionable, ideology or even by serious theory, but also by the acuity of insight of the profoundest philosophers. Even those who disagree with this statement have to admit that the Catholic concept of the State and of politics ought to occupy a place among political theories, a place equal with the others. Particularly in this age of extremist political theorizing, from political positivism to utopian constructs, Catholic realism has a salutary role to play, since it is equidistant from all extreme formulas. In fact, its greatest merit is, precisely, that it proposes no political ideology or myth and recommends no political regime.

Catholic political theory—or politics in the light of Catholic doctrine—is not only shunned in our public and academic discourse, it is presented with a one-sided bias by representatives of the three schools previously mentioned. The authors of the Federalist Papers were understandably far removed from medieval thought and experience, seeing in the Church's functions a manifestation of obscurantism; the two German-American scholars deal not with Catholic *doctrine* but with *heresies* sprung up within the Church's spiritual area: Voegelin with the Abbot Joachim in whom he finds the starting phase of speculative degeneracy, and Strauss with a later phase of the same tendency as manifested in the writings of Machiavelli and Hobbes. Neither thinker devotes any appreciable time and understanding to the study of the Catholic concept of man, as if the heritage of the West that they both celebrate had reached its peak in classical Greece and had degenerated thence. Any valid effort at a reconstruction is conditional, in the view of Strauss and Voegelin, on a return to the classical experience and to the thinkers who best articulated it. Hence, the supernatural element in the make-up of man and political society is entirely overlooked. Its place is taken by natural law, community symbolization, or the philosopher's myth, which are, however, themselves conditional on the free acceptance of the supernatural as an active force in our lives.

This is why we believe in the importance of the endeavor to bring to the American reader's attention *another* tradition, *another* line of thought which is also an integral element of Western political consciousness, although it transcends both the classics and the moderns. The present book is devoted to this endeavor.

Introduction
The Need to View Politics
as a Meaningful Endeavor

We shall try to show in this introduction the need for our contemporaries, especially Christian contemporaries, to understand the nature of politics and the state. To see as clearly as possible, in the light of human experience and Christian teaching, first, that there are constants in the life of communities at every period of history and, second, that in spite of the apparent tumult of political configurations, one can arrive at statements about politics and the state which form a coherent whole. In other words, my argument in the introduction and in the book will be that there is a validly held *Christian-Catholic concept* about these matters, or, if you wish, a Christian-Catholic political theory.

The overall impression of our contemporaries—and "contemporaries" of all ages—concerning political developments tends to be a hopeless confusion, the kind which makes them despair of ever finding orderly lines of force or organizing principles along which events may be comprehended. Such a confusion in our minds, if we let it settle as a definite "view," discourages normal participation in politics or, worse, encourages the wrong participation.[1]

It is not, however, an impossible task to present the reader with an orderly view, provided some conditions are observed. On the following pages, this order is outlined by the organization of chapters: a brief history of political thought from a Christian point of view (first chapter); Christian reflection on the state and politics (second chapter); a discussion of present problems in the light of these reflections, pointing out in particular the errors into which Christian thought on political matters may most naturally fall (third chapter); and a further discussion of the problems of the present, with particular emphasis on how they affect the American scene (fourth chapter).

In this Introduction, two preliminary considerations will be discussed: (a) the *permanence* of politics and political institutions, contrasted with modern attempts to negate them, protest against them, dilute them, and demolish them, and (b) the *changes* that take place, originating from causes one can apprehend and following a course that, with some effort, can be identified not with some abstract "will of history" but with our lives and aspirations.

In spite of the present vogue of general protest against the state, society, family, law, and institutions of all kinds, historically this protest has no basis: all periods knew them and cultivated them. No epoch, no society, no settlement (stable or nomadic) of human beings is known to have existed without the sophisticated development and interaction of these institutions. All efforts to imagine, let alone establish, a state of affairs that would not include them in some form is destined to build castles in the air. Even anarchistic and nihilistic groups, even bands of outlaws recognize stable interrelationships among their members, build these relationships into at least temporarily sets behavior patterns, and establish embryo institutions which officialize and perpetuate these patterns and relationships.

This is why we find that the proliferating ideologies, sects, and movements which declare their programs to change society radically, to render it "more human," more just, loving, fraternal, etc., and thinkers who speak of a social and moral "mutation" very quickly settle in the grooves of habitual, less-than-ideal routine. When such men, armed with a program, establish or take over societies, even entire nations, which they then proceed to transform according to these programs, they do nothing else than exacerbate existing features in the direction of a radicalized evil. There has not been one society, thus "transformed," which does not display an abundance of coercion, despotism, and crime, so that it may be said that the more resplendent and paradisiacal are the promises, the more sharply disappointing will reality prove.

This disappointment is, of course, most obvious in modern totalitarian regimes. One does not have to read the *Gulag Archipelago* to find horrors less spectacular but equally indicative of basic misconceptions and misdirected will in the minds of the leaders concerning society and the state. The Russian mathematical logician, Alexander Zinoviev, describes in his novel, *Radiant Future*,[2] Soviet life *after* de-Stalinization, that is, in the sixties and seventies, as the kind that prevails in a tank of maneater sharks: never a word of truth for fear of spies, never a relaxed moment in the struggle to get to the privileged top, never real friendship and intimacy, because one is always on the alert against blackmail. And this is the situation at the *top* of the social-cultural hierarchy, among academicians, writers, scholars, artists, and professors, who have big apartments and country villas assigned to them, who shop at special stores, at whose disposition there are chauffeur-driven cars, and who travel abroad to congresses. At lower echelons, life is an endless drabness: waiting in lines, poor medical care, ruined family life.

All of this was built, sixty years ago, on the most magnificent promises, indeed of a "radiant future" in which the state would "wither away," each would be provided for according to his need, men and women would be freed from chores and, after a few song-filled hours in factories and offices, would "hunt in the afternoon and write poetry in the evening" (Marx's words).

Or take life in China, during and after Mao. Some of my students claim (most students nowadays, if not completely indifferent, are little ideologues, without critical sense: nonreading, passive receivers of slogans) that only under communism, where "the contradictions of bourgeois-capitalist society have been abolished," can individuals and society act morally. The truth is, in China corruption is rampant at all levels; the "work and reeducation camps" are full, there is a scarcity of all goods, and the police as well as "citizen control" are ever present. More than that: thousands of gangs of youngsters roam the streets of cities and pick fights with the defenseless, whom they rob and murder; they tyrannize their teachers, burning down their homes and at times beating them to death. As one of them, a refugee in Hong Kong, told the American researchers, Ivan and Miriam London, these gangs admire only toughness and cruelty, believe that Hitler and Japanese Admiral Tojo were two of the greatest men because they conquered and shed oceans of blood, and fawn on the memory of Stalin, not because he was the "great benefactor of mankind," as his Western flatterers called him, but because "he wore shiny uniforms and shoulder boards," while Chinese generals "are indistinguishable from foot soldiers." Besides street fighting, the only things these gangs love are Western movies with nude scenes. "We would almost climb on the screen when such pictures were shown."

This is how the carefully planned and constructed (that is, ideology-based) societies turn out to be soon after the initial enthusiasm. Since such constructs are not merely phenomena of our time—which is rich, it is true, in utopian endeavors on a small scale (the hippy communes of California) and on a gigantic one (China, Russia, the countries of Indochina, etc.)—but a constant of history, we will have to analyze them in these pages. Analyze them not only because it is historically observed that when anarchistic principles prevail—in such diverse circumstances as the Anabaptist commune of Thomas Münzer in the early sixteenth century or the utopian settlements in nineteenth-century America—a regime of brutal repression follows, but because Christians, misinterpreting the teaching of their religion, have also indulged in anarchistic and utopian projects. In fact, our third chapter will be devoted to analysis of the false assumption, often made by sincerely religious people, that redeemed man needs no politics; his faith and goodness turn him automatically into an ideal community member and the community, similarly inclined, into a noninstitutional, fraternal place.

It is not sufficient, however, to state that a certain type of intellectual construct in the practical domain of politics is contrary to human nature and to the Church's teaching. Some may argue that if we accept only the status quo as valid and legitimate and reject utopian attempts for change and betterment, we block progress. Such a view is as antinatural as the anarchistic one, since change takes place at all times and is born in the minds of men, as well as arises from new circumstances. Thus we must distinguish between protest against the state, society, law courts, and institutions in general and limited, local criticism against evil forms that such institutions display—against their abuses, their ossification.

As far as transformation and change are concerned, we are witnesses, for example, of many nations' searches for new regimes, new powers for the state, different configurations of society. The reason why we are not readily aware of such contemporary modifications of the political landscape or, if we are, why we tend to diagnose them as temporary aberrations, is that our perspective is limited by older forms which we regard as eternal archetypes. With the phenomenal growth in numbers of students in schools and readers and spectators of communication media, the mass of men, hardly interested in the pursuit of further information, comes to believe that the two or three political systems which now prevail are unchangeable structures. The three systems, let us suggest (with some oversimplification), are communism, democratic liberalism, and socialism, all of which are practiced with some degree of ideological coherence.

To students, newspaper readers, and watchers of television it comes as a shock to learn that these systems—with which they were born—may have reached their zenith, are now on the decline, and are on the point of being replaced by new ones. Even if communism is repulsive for the Western public, it is at least a known, a familiar, reality. The public accepts its existence as it accepts that of an ugly building across from the window, which disfigures the street but is nevertheless part of the habitual field of vision. To tell the citizen that new political configurations are emerging on the horizon is to touch him on a sensitive point: he must part with the familiar landscape, begin thinking of the reasons for the change, and fit into his moral and factual universe a new reality, for whose reception he is not prepared.[3]

Yet the majority of member countries of the United Nations is today in search of what one may call a "third model," roughly equidistant from liberal democracy and communism. These countries may be "rightist" or "leftist," and they may mix their new recipe according to a different dosage, but whether Yugoslavia or Portugal, Afghanistan or Chile, South Africa or the Philippines, they are in the process of liquidating most of the old institutions—parliament, universal suffrage, private property as the leading form of the economy, civilian rule—and are elaborating new institutions. Beyond the somewhat narrow horizon of political textbook writers are authors who challenge the orthodox interpretation of these events and call the new regimes and their policies "national socialistic," not in the sense given this term by Hitler but in recognition of the two principal political inspirations of these regimes: socialism and nationalism.

This is one observable aspect of the transformation; the other is related. Both show clearly that the scholar, and the Christian scholar in his own way and according to his lights, must accept the changing scene not as a chaotic piling up of disconnected events but as a meaningful situation, orderly in its own way and integrable with his worldview. Of course, the work of integration is not without its difficulties.

We have taken cognizance of the contemporary anarchistic protest against the state and institutions, a protest expressed in slogans such as "Society is institutionalized violence," "Institutions are mechanisms of hidden exploitation," "All history is a chronicle of class struggle," "Let imagination take power" (graffiti on the walls of Paris in the spring of 1968), and so on. Whether these watchwords are reactions against too much power accumulated in the hands of the state is hard to tell. It is just as probable that those who launch these slogans aspire to an even greater state power, not in the hands of the "bourgeoisie" but in the hands of the socialist state, conceived as a mild, beneficent, and tolerant fraternity.

Whatever the motives and the consequences, the state has been playing an overwhelming role in the life of nations since the end of the eighteenth century. Hegel had given it a philosophical impetus, one that affected not only the totalitarian but also the democratic regimes. Tocqueville understood the trend also and foresaw, in the United States, what he called the "Tutelary State," an expression we are now justified in translating as the "Welfare State," and whose encompassing power is greater today than even Lord Beveridge imagined possible only thirty-five years ago, when he worked out the Labor Party's program.

Not only German romantics and British laborites but Italian Marxist theoreticians are convinced of the "goodness" of the enormous power that the state is called upon to wield in the new age. Antonio Gramsci, who died in a fascist prison but had there all the intellectual instruments (like Lenin in tsarist exile) with which to elaborate a theory that now seduces many of the best minds on the left *and* right, suggested that the modern state is indeed in the position of Machiavelli's Prince, insofar as the state, an empty but potentially powerful entity, is conquered by the Communist Party, that is, by an intelligent entity that has a history-shaping program and the will to carry it out. And since the Party, as the carrier of history's message, is much more than a mere aggregate of individuals, it is not a mere agency for economic reform but an inspired organizer of morality and intellect. In short, the Party's historic task is to reorganize, intellectually and morally, the state which has integrated in itself (as Hegel had seen) all the citizens.

While Gramsci thus reflected in his prison, his jailer, Mussolini, was writing articles for the *Italian Encyclopedia* with the same theme. The state has a personality, a will; it integrates the citizens with its historic mission; etc. The fact that Mussolini and Gramsci were of the same opinion on this most essential point of politics, the relationship of the state with citizens, shows that the new idea had the backing of a substantial segment of avant-garde political theoreticians and practitioners. Over against the anarchic conditions in liberal-democratic societies—this is the core of the thesis—the state must be restored to a quasi-mystic position. Boris Souvarine, the ex-Communist French biographer of Stalin, relates his conversation in the early twenties with his fellow Communist Preobrazhensky, when the latter tried to have Marx's grandson, Jean Longuet, turn Marx's buried body from Highgate Cemetery over to the Kremlin's rulers for a spectacular reburial. When Souvarine objected to such an act of idolatry (Lenin's body was to be embalmed and exposed in a mausoleum), his comrade dismissed his indignation: "You cannot understand us."

What Souvarine was supposed not to understand was the new cult of the state and its symbols. Thus it was not Stalin, or Hitler, who initiated the so-called "personality cult"; it was embedded in the very nature of the modern state, conceived as a God-substitute by philosophers long before Marx (Thomas Hobbes referred to the state, in his political theory, as "*deus mortalis*").

Can we still hold that the cult of the state should be understood as a reaction to a symmetrical drive toward anarchy, which is equally strongly represented in the modern mind? Or shall we suppose that, historically, the state was always the ultimate expression of the collective power, and that now, after a relatively brief interval of diffuse power (in liberal-democratic regimes), the turn is again back to the monolithic authority of the pharaonic or Inca state? This is what a participant, Liu Hai-t'ao, said at a post-Mao symposium of escaped Chinese intellectuals in Hong Kong in October 1976, a month after Mao died:

> As far as China is concerned, enlightened despotism should not be dismissed completely. At the present stage of development, the Chinese people want to have someone to worship, and Mao understood this perfectly and took full advantage of it.[4]

The answer to our two questions has great importance for political science, and particularly for us in this book. Our preoccupation will be twofold. First, the understanding that, in this imperfect world, changes and even upheavals are normal occurrences but that, throughout the apparent chaos, the constants may be ascertained. In other words, not confusion but order. The second concern is to make it clear that the Christian possesses an incomparable compass in the midst of this tumult: his understanding, inspired by faith and doctrine. This understanding is, above all, of human nature as it struggles under the eyes of Providence. Thus there is a Christian concept of politics and the state which is not the same as a necessarily right action by all Christians: individuals, groups, communities, rulers, or political parties. A Christian theory of politics must be the widest grasp available to man, scholar and practitioner, since the Christian is equidistant from ideologies and their prominent modern forms, anarchy on the one hand and the divinized state on the other.[5] The Christian is equally opposed to the individual's absorption by the community and to the community as a mere contract among individuals. Keeping in mind these political road signs—

those of Christian prudence—we may not err too much in our judgments, perhaps less than is the ordinary lot of men.

For American Catholics, reflection on such guiding lines may have a special importance. The United States made a secular dogma of the separation of state and church(es) before other nations of the West. This step had historical causes, but it was also a practical condition in view of the plurality (later multiplicity) of religions, churches, and sects within American society. Separation seemed to be a good thing, particularly in the eyes of those who did not perceive from the beginning that the "neutrality" of the state, thus its increasingly radical secularization, might sooner or later tempt the representatives of some secular doctrine (ideology) to fill the spiritual void. A "secular religion" was simply not taken into consideration as a probability, perhaps because Americans have been presumptuous enough to think that such a thing "cannot happen here," such a thing being what the "myth of the left" is in France or the "cult of the Party" in other countries, semiofficial but powerfully dictating systems of belief.

Another reason why Americans might reflect usefully on the Christian view of politics is that the state every day penetrates more and more the life of private individuals and private groups, such as educational institutions and, generally, the formation and guidance of the citizens. To be sure, we do not have anything approaching a "cult of the state"; but in practice the state acquires enormous powers over areas where the Church ought to play more than the secondary or insignificant role she is now satisfied to accept. In our increasingly nonmoral society—that is, one in which secular ideologies monopolize the mind—areas where moral teaching and civic decency ought to meet and shoulder the responsibilities together: crime, drugs, premarital pregnancy, child abuse, pornography, the state-formulated remedies, usually gigantic programs that spend millions of dollars but basically are ineffective, remain without religious and moral guidance.

Thus Americans, who have believed thus far in the harmonious coexistence and cooperation of state and Church, may begin to develop a sense of divided loyalty, a new thing in this country. Tocqueville still spoke, in a tone of pleased surprise, about the peace he noted between the representatives of religion, priests and ministers, and the civil authority. This situation, true until quite recently, may soon be modified. Tocqueville also found that the peaceful neighborliness of church and state may guarantee the survival of democracy, because he was convinced that, without the moderating influence of religion, modern democracy, with its ideological content and missionary zeal, may degenerate into a despotic doctrine. The present retreat of the churches from their spiritual tasks, or at least the near liquidation of their moral presence, may leave the state-sponsored secular ideology in a monopolistic and privileged position, so that "democracy" might soon become synonymous with the "pagan state." If that happens, Christians would find themselves, in this progressive century, sharing the fate of their ancestors in the Roman Empire: not necessarily martyrdom and the subsequent triumph, but slow extinction as a religious community.

Here, then, are reasons why the American Christian should pay close attention to such matters as the nature of the state, its relationship to order, freedom, and justice, the meaning of politics, of sovereignty, of the common good, of the Church as above as well as inside society, the share of Church and state in the education of citizens who possess both civic and Christian virtues. In a land where "pluralism" is proudly proclaimed to be the alpha and omega of the community's good life, it is particularly important for Christians to clarify their understanding of the great principles on which the life of men as social beings is based.

Chapter 1
The Catholic View of Political History

There is no better way to grasp the nature of politics than to map an overview of its development in what we call "the West," but which, in reality, includes large sections of the Middle East and North Africa. Why this part of the world, and not China, India, Central Africa, or the lands of the Amerindian empires, of Aztecs and Incas? The answer is not occidentocentric if we consider that these other areas knew at all times only a kind of monolithic rule: usually a divinized king and the caste of his familiars, on one side, and masses of politically undifferentiated slaves or serfs, peasants, and artisans (eventually tradesmen) on the other side. It is in the West, in Mesopotamia and Egypt, that the ruling caste split between the king's Palace and the Temple, not yet rivals but performing different functions: the Temple as a place of worship, center of trade and the distribution of goods, and the Palace as organizer of defense, levier of taxes, enforcer of law and labor.[1]

Political and spiritual power, however, did not diverge to such a degree that various and distinct social classes (strata) should appear, with their own structure and interests, their own ambitions and free-speaking leaders. This development was left to Hellas, with its population living along gulfs, in valleys, and on islands of and around the Aegean Sea, a population actively "commercing," exchanging merchandise and ideas, debating in the marketplace about the good of the city and the happiness of man.

1

Since this debate (which eventually became philosophy) is no concern to us in this chapter, we may focus on the debate about the *polis,* the small and self-contained state. The great political dilemma arose from the very first moment of the *polis:* Who should rule—the best men (*aristoi*), those who possess a stake in the country, namely land and factories and merchant fleets (*oligarchs*), or the assembled people (*demos*)? The great political thinkers and leaders envisaged a mixed regime, fully realizing that even the achieved stability would be fragile, depending on the durability and flexibility of institutions and on the "virtue" of the citizens: their patriotism, spirit of sacrifice for the common good, and freedom with restraint. This is the wisdom of Pericles, as he distilled it in the famous funeral oration for dead Athenian soldiers and as chronicled by the historian of the Peloponnesian War, Thucydides.

Greek political wisdom, which showed a sure grasp of the political dilemma, *including* the grasp that in politics there are no final solutions, was best displayed by Socrates. Condemned (justly? unjustly?) for setting his demanding moral standards higher than those that prevailed in Athenian public life, Plato's teacher refused to flee to safe exile, arguing that towards the end of a life spent in his homeland, whose laws and institutions had shaped and educated him, it would be contradictory for him to escape on the one occasion that the state treated him unjustly.

He drank the poison, thus leaving to posterity the first clear formulation of the many-faceted problem: What is more important, the individual or the state? Can two moralities coexist in the framework of one community? Does the latter possess a personality distinct from that of the citizens? Is there only one moral imperative which state and human person must equally obey? If the state abides by the rules of this moral imperative, can it survive the domestic conflicts, let along external aggression? But is it necessary that the state survive; is a structured state itself an imperative? Yet if it goes under, will the citizens be held together by the mere sociability, or by the mutual interests, of human beings? Are human beings political animals?

These questions (and more) were debated by the Greeks, philosophers and politicans. We see the one central problem: Is the state necessary, and if it is, does it have a life (tradition, interests, rights) of its own? The question is at the core of political life, for the reason that people always

a) Live in organized (instituted) communities,
b) Rebel against its restraints and abuses, yet
c) Are impressed by the state's presence and manifestations of power.

As we said in the Introduction, even protestors against the fact of organized community life, who refer to its deprecatingly as "organized violence," constitute organized communities, just as (the parallel is not far fetched) rebels against Church authority and structure form, from the moment of secession, a new and structured church.[2]

With their analytical and dialectical mindset, the Greeks said almost everything that could be said about the state and the related problems. The West, however, had not completed the fundamentals of political reflection before the Hebrews and Romans shed light on yet other aspects. The Hebrew genius was spiritual whereas the Greek was intellectual. The nation (tribe,? a haphazard group of Semitic slaves cemented together by Moses?) received its stamp and personality, its entire communitarian existence, from Yahweh, who also gave it its "constitution," the Ten Commandments. The lawgivers of Hellas were human beings, although at times legendary, like Sparta's Lycurgus; the Hebrews stood directly under God: the great prophets, his messengers, were endowed with a higher and more unmistakable power than the kings, who more often than not strayed from the righteous path.

Thus the Hebrews were a nation and a state, to be sure, but just as essentially, their community was divinely ordained, and as such it was more than a state. This ambiguity later exacerbated the ambiguous Greek heritage, and sharpened the Western political self-questioning: Should the state be moral and politics follow divine dictates? Does God's representative (the prophet, Christ, the pope) have preeminence, in matters of worldly power, over the king? After all, while the Greeks invested only human beings (legislators, assemblies) with political and constitutional powers, the Hebrews obtained their political rules ready made (the Tablets) and worded in such moral-religious terms that their political interpretation, had it been necessary, would have been arduous and forever controversial. Of course, it *was* to remain so—in the West.

To Greek *philosophical* analysis and Hebrew stress on power's *spiritual* roots and nature, the Romans added the elaborate idea of *law* as the organizing principle of statecraft. Perhaps the best comment on the essence of the Roman political genius, at least before the time of Caesar and Cicero, came from the pen of Polybius, the Greek observer of Rome's rise to power, who wrote in the course of its fifty-three years, admiringly but puzzled. Polybius admired the Romans' practical wisdom of creating a mixed regime, which in Hellas remained only the philosopher's dream. The mixed constitution was held together, according to the Greek historian, by the fact that Roman democracy (the term is not to be taken in its modern sense) did not disorganize the nation as it did elsewhere (among the Greeks, for example) but was strengthened by *pietas,* the worship of the gods, the honor paid to parents and respect to elders, and by obedience to the laws (book VI). Yet Polybius was Greek enough to suggest that, beyond these positive elements, Roman grandeur was to be attributed to the intangible Fortune (*tyché*) which stands above individuals and nations, and which the good statesman includes in his calculations—precisely because it represents the incalculable.

> Tyché produces for ever something new, but never before did it produce such a show-piece: the rise of

> Rome to world dominion from 220 to 167. Here tyché
> seems to have worked for a definite goal.[3]

Although Polybius observed Rome at the height of republican power, he never discounted (again as a true Greek thinker) the factors that were already working toward decadence and fall. Even mixed constitutions must decline, he submitted, and he saw the signs around him: corrupted youth, venality of power, extravagant ambition in leading men, unlimited demagogy in competition for high political office. In the circles of his eminent friends (the household of the Scipio family), the guests debated the necessity of a "constitutional magistracy" in order to check the growing disorder. Later, but still in republican times, others discussed the state's right to intervene in private affairs and offend the right to private property.

In other words, as Polybius foresaw it, although he based his view on the Greek concept of the cyclical rise and collapse of all things, Rome was slowly ceasing to be a mixed regime and was evolving toward a strong and centralized state power, represented by a magistrate with constitutional but vast powers. Their role was cut out for the caesars, not merely as rulers of Rome (they never ceased calling it a "republic") but also as "universal" rulers, in the name of the statecraft than which no better might be conceived by men.

There are some conclusions to be drawn from the aforementioned observations. The fact of the state is at all times and places taken for granted, no less in the more loosely organized Western lands than in what we call "monolithic" empires in the rest of the world. The specificity of the Western mind enters the great political debate on the issues of state versus the spiritual authority (Hebrews), the ethical nature of the state (mixed regime) and the right balance between state and citizens (Hellas), and the growth of the state due to the citizens' virtues and cooperation,

which poses the question of a centralized power (Rome).
Everywhere, also, spectacularly since the case of Socrates, the
dilemma known under the label *raison d'état* begins to be articulated: whether the state possesses the right to override the rights
and interests of the citizens in view of superior interests, which
remain eventually undisclosed to the public. As in the United
States, when it was asked in the Nixon/Watergate controversy:
Does the ruler, although bound by laws, stand above the law in his
pursuit of what he perceives as the good of the nation?

The Greek thinkers debated all these questions and their
theoretical treatises summarized for posterity the great issues
of politics. Since Christian thinkers were to consult them closely,
the Greeks conclusions are crucial for the basic formulations
of both the Christian Middle Ages and modern times.

It is enough for our purposes to consult Aristotle, mainly because his thought penetrated most deeply into Christian
thought, through the mediation primarily of Thomas Aquinas.
Man, above all else a rational being, seeks happiness—which for
Aristotle is not the mere enjoyment of worldly advantages but a
harmonious development that we call the "good life." Man finds
the optimal conditions for the achievement of happiness in the
polis, a kind of extrapolated state of harmony—although, as
Aristotle was well aware, rarely without conflicts, upsets, and
violent changes of regimes. Nonetheless, as Cicero was to echo
most succinctly, men aggregate naturally:

> It is less their weakness [which drives them to it] than
> the innate need to be in the company of their likes.
> Man is not made to live isolated, in solitude. Even
> when surrounded with riches, his nature urges him to
> assemble with others.[4]

Aristotle insisted on this point repeatedly; only superhumans,
or subhumans, may live "without a hearth, without class, without

laws" (as, for example, the monster Cyclops in the Homeric tale). Ordinary men are never stateless: "The State itself is an association of families and villages in a perfect and self-sufficient existence, that is a life of true felicity and goodness" (*Politics,* book III). Thus the state is not optional, it is a necessity, and therefore a good thing for man since he possesses reason, by which he discerns the best means to become happy and acquire fullness. Aristotle continues:

> The State exists not merely that men may live but that they may live well.... Whence it is plain that a State which is truly and not superficially so called, must be concerned with virtue: otherwise, a political community degenerates into a mere alliance [book III, 9].

A passage of great consequence, because it contains the grain of tremendous future debates: Is the state to be concerned with, and therefore teach, virtue, or should it be (Aristotle writes "degenerate into") a mere framework, a contractual arrangement among individuals, choosing or not choosing to be virtuous? Catholic teaching will be unmistakably on the side of the Greek sage, but not without an all-important correction by St. Thomas: membership in the state means, of course, a high degree of integration by the citizens. Nevertheless, man is not ordered exclusively, and with all his being, to the good of the state. Most of his acts may even be indifferent as regards the state, neither harmful nor virtuous; that is, without any political significance (St. Thomas's *Preface* to Aristotle's *Politics*).[5] An essential distinction, since Aristotle also wrote: "The citizen ought not to think that he belongs to himself, but that all belong to the *polis;* each is a part of the City, and the parts should be treated only in view of the whole" (*Politics,* book VIII, 1). For the Christian, however, the highest good is not attainable in and through the state but in and through communion with Jesus Christ. There is a part of man that is not subordinated to the community. The christian concept is opposed to the diminishing of the individual that would make of him a means toward an end, even if this end is the common good. Yet, following St. Paul, Thomas does not teach hostility, not even indifference, vis-à-vis the state. In fact, in contrast to St. Augustine, he maintained that had Adam not sinned, human beings would nonetheless live in a political community.

At other places in the *Politics,* Aristotle too was moderate in setting down the limits of the state, criticizing Plato for his monolithic state structure in *The Republic.* There is a degree of unity of the state, Aristotle said in book II, beyond which the state would cease to be a state, that is, the converging point of a healthy plurality. This is implicitly admitted when he argues for adjustment of the constitution to existing situations in which people live. Thus the "good" constitution, hence good laws, are not the same for Greeks and barbarians, not even for the various Greek states—a distant foundation of the thesis, later accepted by the Church, that there is no such thing as an "ideal regime," hence no precisely formulated "Catholic politics."[6] Naturally, such a position is not to the liking of all Catholics, who argue, on the left and on the right, that the Church, explicitly or at least implicitly, endorses this or that regime, this or that political configuration or party. (Of this, more in subsequent passages.)

Christianity has had an enormous, still-lasting impact on the destinies of politics and political thought. Whether Greek or "barbarian," all states had thus far assumed that the citizen is fully integrated with the community, which means the gods of the community too. To be sure, the ancients distinguished the good man and the bad, yet their conception of the political fact did not go beyond life lived in, and acquiring meaning from, the compact aggregate: tribe, *polis,* monolithic empire. The greatest thinkers of Hellas struggled in their speculation against the limits thus imposed on man's potential transcendence; however, none got far enough. The "good man" could become "divine," but this meant only the contemplative and ascetic qualities, as well as purification from lowliness and greed (Socrates). Thus, for example, a slave could not become a "good man" since his condition of life condemned him to base work and a quasi-animal status.

Only the Hebrews distinguished between the political community and the ethical life, but not even their religious capacity was able to contain the idea of separation into the City of God and the this-worldly human community. Yahweh took a very close interest in Hebrew political (even military) affairs; the Jew (the prophet) had, it is true, the dubious status (although not the explicit right) of standing aside and reproaching the king and the whole nation for straying from God's path, but a return to that path meant only the betterment of the Hebrew people as a unit, not an individual aspiration to special merit.

Christianity, on the other hand, recognized two kingdoms, with the consequence that the human person could now appeal from the first to the second. Since one of the chief attributes of any state is its monopoly on rendering justice,[7] the Christian notion of a worldly and a divine tribunal meant a kind of "dual citizenship." The ancient state could not countenance this, its conceptual framework being unable to grasp the individual of divided loyalty. And in fact, just this issue, divided loyalty, has plagued political thought throughout Christian times, with many thinkers unwilling to accept it and trying to recapture the unitary idea of the state in pagan times.

It took three centuries for the pagan (Roman) state to digest the ineluctable fact of Christianity, that is, first of all, the idea that the citizen is "not chained to a system of beliefs by his birth and life in a given community."[8] For three hundred years this was one of the main charges against Christians, namely, that they were by definition and by choice bad citizens, recognizing only one king, Jesus Christ, and refusing to sacrifice to the statue of the emperor. Tertullian argued most eloquently against this accusation, but to no avail. He said that according to Christian belief, all power is derived from God. Thus "we, Christians, acknowledge in Caesar God's choice; we pray for him and respect him. He is in a way more ours than yours, since it is our God who placed him on his throne." And it is true that, as another, even earlier document, the *Epistle to Diognetes,* testifies, Christians proved themselves good citizens and soldiers in all instances, since for them the state was a divine creation, remaining essentially just even in persecutions.[9]

If, nevertheless, Rome ended up by coopting the Christian religion, then making of it the state religion, this was done for two reasons: parallel to Christianity, other systems of thought and belief (Stoicism and various Oriental creeds) had penetrated Roman private life and brought about a general softening of attitudes. Paganism was no longer, in the fourth century, a collection of empty rites, performed for the state, but a world conception, with the notion of a future life. The same moral sphere was now valid for both paganism and Christianity, so that one could pass from one to the other without great shocks.[10] In other words, pagan thought had not remained stagnant from the Platonist Cicero to the converted Constantine; it had absorbed a great many new elements. When the emperor smoothed the way toward the reconciliation of Christianity, he had recognized the reality of a certain convergence.

The second reason for coopting the Church was political. Constantine, like all Romans, mixed a shrewd realism with superstitions. Before the evident decline, he was determined to win the favor of the Christians' God by bringing about the cooperation between Church and state and by granting considerable powers to the bishops and clergy, so that they might lend new vigor to a flabby bureaucracy. This was perhaps an inevitable measure, but it had grave consequences. In the ancient pagan religions the priests had no political role or influence; the Temple, as we saw, had been overcome and assimilated by the king's Palace. This was even more true of Rome. With Christianity, the ecclesiastical class, invited by Constantine and his successors, penetrated the government, strengthening it by the Church's tight organization. The Church versus state issue was not to disappear for the remainder of the Christian centuries; indeed it is still with us.

The new Roman-Christian Empire received its greatest political summation from St. Augustine. He had to answer those (still many) pagans who saw in the sack of Rome by the Gothic king, Alaric (410), a proof that the gods had deserted the city and that the Christian God was unable to protect it. Augustine's counterarguments are contained in *The City of God,* a work which set down the lines of thought for a thousand years of Christian political speculation.

Augustine, if we wish to situate him with regard to Greek philosophy, was a Platonist, without any sort of Aristotelian element in his thinking. As Plato had elaborated the system of two worlds of cognition, ideas and their mundane copies, Augustine distinguished two cities, of the just and the unjust men. In later medieval interpretation, the heavenly city came to be identified with the Church, the earthly city with the state.[11] The latter was conceived as a mostly coercive and greedy mechanism, its leaders robber barons, its citizens (by definition) non-Christian men. Christians submit to Caesar but only as Christ submitted to Pilate, their better part refusing mundane domination. Thus politics is evil, except when the Church, a representative of the *civitas Dei,* if not indeed its incarnation here below, receives support from the state. Then the latter is able to administer justice in a situation where the two cities intermingle.

It is questionable whether Augustine's grandiose book, the first by a Christian on political philosophy, was accepted by pagan intellectuals as an answer to their reflections, dictated by the great changes. It is more important that the book supplied arguments for those who later were to be passive before the state they regarded as almost entirely evil, a punishment of God for mankind's sins, thus at best a necessary evil. This was, to a large extent, "Protestant" thought on politics, and this thought has remained its axis to this day. The alternative to the state (*is* there an alternative?) was Christian life, which, even if it is powerless here below to secure peace and a God-fearing government, ensures the peace of the Christian's soul.

Augustinism is thus an essentially apolitical system of thought, often feeding the Christian's utopian aspirations for a world that lives by faith and goodness, a heavenly city established on earth, even though surrounded by evil men and monstrous empires. Men who live in grace do not need state and government, or, at most, they accommodate themselves with a government that is directly of God. One may readily see how such an aspiration encourages pacifism, dismantlement of the state and its institutions, and creation of a "world government" of God's elect who belong exclusively to the heavenly city.

The Christian Middle Ages received a brilliant but difficult heritage. Simplifying matters, we can say that the political issue in ancient times centered around the state, which existed as an unproblematic entity, propitiating the municipal pantheon, and sure of its citizens' devotion (or at least obedience), since they too depended on the good will of the same gods.[12] Christianity turned this stable arrangement upside down. First of all, there were now two spheres, the spiritual and the temporal, and thus two supreme ruling and governing entities, Church and state. Both were divinely willed and created. Second, their relationship was full of conflicts of a historical, theological, and finally political nature. And third, the very fact of these conflicts created circumstances in which new entities could emerge, allied now to the state against the Church, then to Church against state—until such time when these new entities—feudal lords, early communes, burghers, humanists, clerics—became self-reliant and entered the fray on their own.

Let us turn now with closer attention to the second point, the relationship between state (king, emperor) and Church (pope, bishops, religious orders, outstanding abbots).

With the fall of the Western Roman Empire, the papacy also suffered a certain eclipse; in fact, it was afterward for centuries surrounded by hostile forces, taking advantage of the Church's political weakness and the fact that, under the protection of the Eastern emperors, some powerful patriarchs in Constantinople all but challenged the authority of the Bishop of Rome. An unexpected but well-seized opportunity presented itself for Rome when Pepin and Charlemagne became powerful rulers of the Franks; the latter decisively defeated the Lombards, who had threatened central Italy, and had himself crowned by the pope at Christmas, 800. Two consequences are noteworthy. The idea of the Roman Empire again materialized in the West, under Charlesmagne and his successors, then under a long line of German "holy Roman" emperors; and the Church, under periodically emerging strong pontiffs, Gregory VII, Innocent III, Boniface VIII, was able to become the equal, even the superior partner of the emperors in governing and inspiring the Christian world, the *respublica christiana*.

Since politics penetrates every part of human relationships, that between the two heads of the medieval Christian world did not remain foreign to politics either. The problem which now presented itself—and did not go away until the eclipse of the papacy as a worldly power in the sixteenth century—was the following. At the beginning, in the centuries between the eighth and the eleventh, the secular power prevailed, due partly to the emperor's prestige, partly to the emerging feudal system, both now feared and respected by a populace that had been saved from the turbulent times of barbarian invasions. With the settling of people inside the new order, and thanks to papal authority, a renaissance of ecclesiastical power occurred, clearly noticeable in the Gothic art forms where God's greatness is celebrated in stone and stained glass. Contrary to the style of celebration in the Eastern empire (in art, for example, in the mosaics of Ravenna), where the emperor is depicted as a semidivine figure, emperors and kings in the West are represented as receiving their powers from God and as standing hierarchically under the celestial ranks. A late echo of this state of things may be perceived in the writings of Bishop Bossuet at the zenith of royal absolutism, in the seventeenth century:

> The power of kings comes from above, yet they must not think that they are masters of this power, using it at their whim; they are compelled to use it with fear and moderation, since God will demand an account. [And even more forcefully:] Kings must tremble while using their God-given powers, and think how horrible is the sacrilege of using such a power for evil.[13]

Two factors were at work from about the thirteenth century to weaken the ecclesiastical hold. Ultimately, they were to result in what Georges de Lagarde, author of a vast synthesis of late medieval thought, calls the "birth of the lay spirit."[14] The first drive originated in the midst of the religious orders, the so-called mendicant orders. Although conceived as Christian militias and servants of the Church (they indeed fulfilled this role), they became quasi-independent centers of speculation, conduct, artistic representation, and, importantly for us here, focuses of thought on the relationship with the secular world. This is how art and social historian Georges Duby describes this evolution:

> Through sermons, through theatrical representations, through various means of direct action,

the mendicant orders began to detach the faithful from the Church, conceived as a rival. They reinvigorated the anti-clerical tendencies of the heretical movements, the same ones they had had the mission to combat and rally to the orthodoxy, and whose resurgence they now blocked.[15]

Among these mendicant orders, and especially the Franciscans (or rather a branch, the so-called Fraticelli), some began to challenge essential doctrines of the Church, in which they proved unsuccessful. But other Franciscans, such as William of Ockham, succeeded in formulating and accrediting the notion that the secular ruler need not submit to the spiritual power—that, in other words, secular power has no religious basis.[16]

With this statement we have named the second factor which was to weaken the Church's position of supremacy in the Christian West. The medievel question, whence the state's power? received various answers. The feudal lords: From the power of the sword, from wars. The doctors of the Church: It is God who delegates their power to kings. The pope: Power comes from God, but through the mediation of St. Peter and his successors.

If we discount the first answer as not within the scope of Christian speculation, we still find deep controversy between the other two propositions—and, as we shall see, a third one—both of which invoke God as the source of royal or imperial power. God delegates his powers, but does he do so via the Church (pope) or directly? After all, there was the Roman Empire, a pagan empire, into which Christ and the apostles were born and which they accepted (one of them, Paul, was a citizen of it). Long before Peter was born, there were emperors and empires; thus temporal rule can be said to antedate the Church, to be equal with it in power and independence, both depending, although through separate channels, directly on God's creation and sustaining will.[17]

This debate was not only theological, it cut into the flesh of high political interests as well as daily affairs. Its various interpretations meant a positive or a negative answer to such questions as whether, for reasons of *political* disobedience, the pope had the right to excommunicate the emperor; whether the bishops had the right to independent secular possessions and dominations, even privileges; whether members of the clergy may have recourse to ecclesiastical courts; and so on. The secular side in these and other matters came to be represented by the new class of lawyers who studied Roman law at the new University of Bologna and by such theologian-legalists as William of Ockham and Marsilius of Padua. In combination—that is, of the theological and historical/legal arguments—they were validating the emperor's cause, and ultimately the cause of secularization.

From the enormous literature generated by this network of conflict and controversy we can attempt to disengage only a few major themes. The most important was the trend to oppose the Church's power and ubiquitous influence by referring to the original, "evangelical" poverty (upheld by the radical Franciscans and the heretical sects) and by the effort to rehabilitate the Roman concept of law and state as an alternative to the prevailing mode of thought. The first issue never received a "solution," though it was to be taken up by the reformers who criticized the Church's wealth, pomp, and ceremony. It was the second issue which grew into an enormous tidal wave, since all sorts of interests and aspirations found themselves represented in it.

No question that the lawyers carried the major part of the attack against the Church's secular power and ecclesiastical property: they represented the aggressive drive of secularization of Frederick II, the Hohenstaufen emperor; of the French kings, relieved of imperial pressure at the death of Frederick; of the Italian communes, which wanted to impose town taxes and their own jurisdiction on the clerics; and so on. These issues received theoretical support from the political thinkers and the early humanists. The first argued, with Aristotle, that the state is a natural thing; that the emperor receives the power of the sword from God (Simon of Bisignano, end of the twelfth century); that the king, even if crowned by a priest, still governs a human institution (Ockham, early fourteenth century); etc. The second, the humanists, did not put forth arguments but studied the ancient political and legal literature of Rome, and concluded that that society (the pagan Roman society) was purely secular, yet well ordered and efficiently governed. They went even further when they discovered (in the second-century Roman jurist, Ulpian) that the public law in Rome referred also to sacred things and that priests were appointed to what amounts to civil service, "civil" and "sacred" being naturally confused in Roman public philosophy. Thus reference to Roman law had the effect of releasing "the Christian ruler from ecclesiological encumbrances by secularizing his government's fundations."[18]

According to Walter Ullmann's somewhat exaggerated thesis, the consultation of ancient literature was prompted by the twin ambition to desacralize the religious man—to restore, as he puts it, the original, pre-Christian, unregenerated man—and to restore as well the concept of politics as an independent category of thought and area of action. He states his conviction that the *studia humanitatis*, that is, humanism before and during the Renaissance, was not more than an auxiliary science in this endeavor, really an outgrowth of the attempts to secure for the ruler his emancipation from ecclesiastical tutelage. While this is an exaggeration, the fact is that a man who was both a humanist and a student of law, Marsilius of Padua, effected the final junction between the various opponents of the Church's power. His treatise, *Defensor Pacis*, has a deceptively simple thesis: The "peace" that must be defended is that of the entire Christian community, threatened by the Church's claim to spiritual authority. But Christ gave the Church no "power of the keys"; he was no "king of kings"; therefore the pope should have no secular power either. The pope is a mere usurper, even in his claim to rule over the clergy. Instead, priests *and* popes ought to be subject to election by the people; they should be subject to secular power. For after all, the Christian community as a whole is the only reliable legislator, judge, and interpreter of doctrine. The "spiritual power" is a dangerous device for splitting the community; all power is vested in the people and their elected rulers.

One can see, even from this brief summary, that Marsilius stood at the dead center of diffuse radical doctrines which preceded his time and the better-identifiable political theories afterward—those of Machiavelli, Hobbes, and Rousseau, with their "civil religion"—up to our own radical critics of the spiritual authority. Such theses were put forward, as we said, by the emperors' and kings' lawyers, partly to safeguard the secular ruler's theoretical power base. In this endeavor, the lawyers were justified. But with Marsilius and others who came later, the legitimate self-defense of the secular ruler against ecclesiastical encroachment degenerated into an *ideology,* a radical affirmation of a cause and an enterprise of demolition of the other cause.

The issue which had arisen with the birth of Christianity, Is man a citizen of *two* realms, instead of the tangible, secular realm only? received from these thinkers an indignantly negative answer: The political community excludes all others; what is called "spiritual" must be equally determined and articulated by the secular power. This is, in essence, the basis of "modernist" political thought, a "civil religion," the ideology of the community, organized by and for the community, a denial of transcendence. Hence the infatuation with the pagan state, ancient for the medieval lawyers, modern with contemporary ideologues. Hence the exaltation of the ruler (by Marsilius, Machiavelli, Hobbes, etc.) and his endowment with absolute power.

Marsilius is popularly credited with the "conciliar thesis," namely, that real power in the Church should not belong to the pope, not even to any segment of the clergy, but to the representatives of all Christendom, assembled in council. Nor should the pope have the monopoly of calling together such an assembly; only the emperor should have that power, and the results of the deliberations should have a binding effect on the pope. It is obvious, however, that the objective of Marsilius is not the establishment of a mere ecclesiastical democracy but, far beyond that, the creation of a kind of totalitarian rule in which people's spiritual aspirations may flow through only one channel: the one determined by the ruler—that is, in the modern sense of the word, by the state. As G. de Lagarde writes,

> Up to Marsilius, nobody thought of denying the reality of a spiritual power and to contest its competence in the properly religious domain. It was Marsilius's own contribution to negate the very existence and possibility of a spiritual power.[19]

In spite of the radicalism of Marsilius and his ideological mind, we must be very careful in discerning the various motives of his attacks against the Church, as well as similar attacks by others. There was the ubiquity of Church penetration into secular life, which irritated the powerful and analytical minds, nurtured precisely by the institutions of the Church. There was the often strained relationship, reminiscent of feudal relationships, between the Church and the various religious orders, now extremely powerful, quasi-independent centers of power. This developed at times into a competition not only between Church and religious order but among the orders themselves, each claiming for its mission and functions a specially exalted status. There was the role of secular rulers and the strong towns, now independent sources of power and influence, and their taking sides in—more, influencing—the ecclesiastical rivalries. And there was, not least, the desire of Italian patriots, among them members of the clergy, to weaken the pope's secular power in the peninsula, to incite the emperor to fight the pope and thus achieve the liberation and unification of Italy as a non-Church-dominated state. Both William of Ockham and Marsilius at one point sought refuge at the court of Emperor Louis of Bavaria, and when Ockham took up his pen in defense of the latter's cause, it was as a representative of antipapal Franciscans *and* as a philosophical exponent of the ruler's secular base.

Such men achieved an easy popularity in the eyes of posterity. It may seem, indeed, that their ambition was eminently human and reasonable, even genuinely spiritual, for the good of the Church and that of the state. The impression we form of their life work is that they aimed, first of all, at *separating* what was previously if not united at least intertwined by historical contingencies, such as the temporal and the spiritual spheres, and at *safeguarding* the function and independence of both. They are supposed to have proposed ways of purifying religion, cutting away the weeds, such as power hunger, accumulation of wealth, interference and conflict with secular interests. Thus Professor A. S. McGrade argues that William of Ockham merely advocated "a less juridical and more spiritual ecclesiastical government,"[20] and Professor Alan Gewirth that Marsilius gave only an early outline of a democratic regime.[21]

The truth is much more complex, and perhaps less favorable to the family of thinkers represented by the professors. Ockham's philosophy was subjectivist, the kind that medieval Scholastic terminology called "nominalistic." Even Professor McGrade, otherwise a partisan of Ockham, admits that this subjectivity had the effect of depriving politics of a theological, and we might add, rational foundation.

What does this mean? Nominalism rejects the real existence of the so-called universals; it proposes, in other words, that there is no such thing as mankind, only individual men and women—no such thing as friendship, only friendly attitudes between two or more persons. If that is so, then state, Church, corporations, institutions, etc., are not *real* either; politics is reduced to empirically observable acts that the weakness of our mind tends to group under names, which, however, remain empty of contents (*flatus vocis*). Thus the proper actors of the political sphere are concrete individuals with here-and-now interests, not corporate wholes. It follows that the area of politics is exclusively that of the secular power, whose motions and motives can be empirically ascertained, and that the spiritual authority has no place in it. The king's power is conferred by men who see to it that the minimal goals of secular government are attained, and they are generally successful in so doing because king and subjects are reasonable people.

Ockham, of course, was a religious man. He recognized the specificity of spiritual power, which, although it has no empirical basis, is appointed by God. It is on God's will, on revelation and on the Bible, that spiritual authority rests, and this was enough to validate it in Ockham's eyes. But suppose a man comes along less pious than the great Franciscan thinker, a Marsilius, for example. He will not do more than pay lip service to the Bible, thus removing any and all justification of spiritual power. The latter remains dangling, and not only is it subordinated to the empirically verifiable secular sphere, its specificity is denied and confiscated for the secular sphere in the form of a secular/spiritual religion—that is, as we say today, an "ideology."

This was the consequence of the many-pronged movement to emancipate the state from Church interference. The question now is, Did the attack on spiritual power, in itself and for its role in the secular area, not also erode the status of the temporal power, the state? At first sight, it seems that the state, as such, had been the winner of the conflict. As John of Paris saw it, the rulership did not function by the effluence of grace; therefore there was no need for the priest's mediating role: everything the political realm needed was already there. Government belonged to the natural community, the state. As creator of nature, God had endowed nature with its own laws, one of which concerns the establishment of the state and its government. Nothing was left that could be mediated. As far as the Church was concerned, the same John of Paris logically held, it was a *purely mystical* body, having nothing to do with the *purely natural* body politic. The function of its ministers is not half political, it is exclusively sacramental.

We should argue, naturally, and will do so at a greater length in the next chapter, that the *separation* effected by such medievals thinkers as Simon of Bisignano, William of Ockham, John of Paris, Marsilius of Padua (and others) weakened the status of the spiritual authority, but that it also undermined the power of the very state that the separation was to make independent of the spiritual. One thing to be considered is that no community can stand unless the spiritual element (which is also the civilizing element) is integrated with its existence and structure. The secular state as such, whether the medieval or the modern, the liberal or Marxist, is able to generate only an ersatz spirituality (ideology), which works not at its preservation but at its destruction. However, the other issue, at this point of our historical-political analysis, is that the concept of the state suffered at the hands of those whose aim had been to strengthen it.

What kind of concept of the state was elaborated by the emperors' and kings' partisans? The citizens were assumed to be men of reason and justice and, as Marsilius had it, their assemblies were supposed to constitute the surest body of legislators—to such an extent that they were also to legislate the correct interpretation of doctrine, this time as assemblies of believers. Following Marsilius, Wyclif, who was also an opponent of the visible Church, suggested that churchmen should enter the ruler's sphere of obedience and that only the ruler possesses the right to exclude (that is, excommunicate) any member from what would then be a spiritualized (ideological) community. The question is: Can the state, saddled with spiritual or quasi- or pseudo-spiritual responsibilities, remain a state? Did the predecessors and followers of Marsilius not grant the state a poisoned gift when they radicalized its function beyond all measure? Perhaps they thought they were putting an end to a grievous mixture of rules and responsibilities with the far-reaching separation of Church and state. But the flaw in their thinking was evident when they conceived the Church as a purely mystical body (John of Paris), thus the state as governing the secular domain but with powers too heavy for it to shoulder.

The second flaw was of a purely political character. On the surface and in good faith, the beneficiary of the changes should have been the secular ruler. The monarchic principle was taken for granted by medieval thinkers, leaning on both the biblical and the classical precepts in this area and also on the Roman precedent. Even Bishop Bossuet was to write in the seventeenth century that Rome ought not have abolished its kingdom and turned into a republic, because, after several hundred years, it proved that much harder to return to the monarchy, that of the caesars. Yet was it the ruler (the state) whose position was now strengthened, at the end of the conflict between spiritual and temporal? In practice and for a while, yes; but the theoretical undermining proceeded apace. Not only was the ruler to be elected by the people, the laws too were the expression of the people's will. And since the people follow their natural desires, they cannot enact laws which are unjust! Nature itself restricts the bad exercise of popular sovereignty! (Marsilius). The same naturalism (and optimism) in Ockham: "natural equity" suffices to regulate human affairs if (!) men live reasonably.

Insensibly, then, the "defense of peace" (from the meddling of the spiritual authority) became a contradictory position: the secular state was divided between ruler and people, an ambiguous division since the first no longer had a spiritual authority behind him, while the second did not have the instruments (for exam-

ple, democratic representation) to make its will known. With all
its imperfections, the earlier system was at least coherent: the
people were united by the Christian faith, represented and
guided by a visible Church, and they were governed by a ruler
who shared their faith. In the proposed dispensation, the *consent*
was left either to the ruler's ability to enforce Christianity or any
other system of belief (an enforced consent) or to the "rea-
sonableness" of the citizens' agreeing, in their "natural equity,"
to legislate for the public good.

What I have described was for several centuries the development
of political thought, particularly about the state. Meanwhile,
another formulation was effected, for the better understanding
of which this background is necessary. This formulation of
state and politics was mainly the work of Thomas Aquinas in
the middle of the thirteenth century. The problem, as he
saw it, was not primarily the conflict between Church and
state but clarification of the nature of the state, its ground in
divine or human will. The fundamental analysis of the political
phenomenon took Thomas back to Aristotle, to whose conclusions he added his own Christian insights. In the Greek
philosopher's view, the *polis* was a great good for man but not
the highest good, which is the spiritual and moral value of the
citizens. Thomas located the highest good in Christian life,
which the state should not obstruct but rather promote. Thus
the state remains a secondary good, and it is ordained for the
good life of all, not only Christians. Natural reason is enough for
citizenship, and natural reason operates without any revelation
or grace: it is not *ratio fide informata* (reason permeated by faith).
Nature, thus, follows its own laws when establishing the state for
the good of all, since in it human reason expresses itself to full
extent. *Per se* and in its own place, the state is a *communitas
perfectissima* for the realization of man's faculties, although, and
this must be emphasized, it is only an intermediate, not a final,
end.

An intermediate end but not something left to human choice. When it is suggested (by anarchists or libertarians) that either man does not need the state or that the state is established by a contract which is revokable, it is assumed that man is, as Aristotle said, not human but a saint or a beast. The human being, precisely because he is rational, cannot exist without a structured community (a possible definition of the state). When it is argued that the foundation of the state lies in a contract, it is overlooked that the potential contractants themselves, before they sit down to agree, would already have sophisticated political concepts in their minds, as well as political experience and wisdom, in order to elaborate the contract. Thus the "contract theory of the state" leaves out of account the fact that it implies an infinite regression to previous (hypothetical) contracts. What is true in this matter, however, is that a *kind* of contract may be assumed, for the sake of speculative convenience, in the foundation of this or that *concrete* state. Even if, historically, things did not and do not take such a course, it can be argued that it is the will of the citizens to organize a given state.

This is how we come to Thomas's view of the controversy. It is clear from what has been said about natural reason that political society is not to be equated with a community that is based on the rule of grace, hence on ecclesiastical overlordship. In fact, only the ruler rules by divine grace. Thus Thomas comes out in favor of the secular ruler's authority, unimpeded by ecclesiastical interference. On the other hand, even though the state ought not legislate virtue, and law can forbid only such deeds that are directed against community life, the life of the state is a process of education of the citizen. Thomas's thought is very subtle on this point:

> Human laws do not forbid all vices from which the virtuous abstain, but only the more grievous vices from which it is possible for the majority to abstain; and chiefly those that are to the hurt of others, with-

out the prohibition of which human society could not
be maintained. . . . The purpose of human law is to
lead men to virtue, not suddenly but gradually.
Wherefore it does not lay upon the multitude of imperfect men the burdens of those who are already
virtuous, namely that they should abstain from all
evil. Otherwise, these imperfect ones, being unable to
bear such precepts, would break out into yet greater
evils.[22]

Several things follow from this passage, pertaining to our discussion. The first is, and Thomas leaves no doubt about it in
our mind, that the functioning of the state presupposes a strong
authority, preferably a monarch.[23] The second is that the
monarch should be a secular ruler, not a priest, who would make
grace and virtue his governing principle. The third thing to
keep in mind is that virtue and the efforts to lead people to
virtue are the main tasks of the state, something that Thomas
did not imagine can be done without the active presence and
participation of Church institutions.[24] At this point he implicitly
contradicts those who favor a "civil religion," because such a
creed would have nothing to do with Christian but only with
"national" virtues. The fourth thing is that Thomas did not and
could not propose democracy or the sovereignty of the people,
since he saw clearly that the majority is never virtuous, and yet
virtue is the *telos,* or formative element, of the community.

At what point does Thomas include the people as an active
factor in political life? We saw that the reforms preached by
Pope Gregory VII at the end of the eleventh century gave rise to
two popular movements, the heretical sects and soon, to counter
their influence, the mendicant orders. There were other signs
also of the inclusion of the masses of people in the rudiments of
political life: the Crusades, the recognition extended to the
towns, the building of vast cathedrals, and the passion plays,

which integrated all Christians with the life of the ecclesiastical community. The heretical sects, Ullmann writes, "assumed importance less by virtue of their tenets, as by virtue of their character as movements embodying the spirit of a revolting multitude against the contemporary form of Christianity,"[25] which was impregnated with the spirit of feudalism, not only in secular life but also in the Church.

It is not our task here to examine the theological errors of these sects, but to point out that they arose, in the eleventh and twelfth centuries, in places which were economically and culturally advanced over the rest of Christendom: in the Rhine Valley, in northern Italy, and in Provence. Thus they recruited not only among the inevitable "marginal" elements of society but also among the rich merchants (for example, Peter Valdo, founder of the Waldensians) and the lower echelons of the corporations. In other words, these sects also had a political aspect, and if their main expression was in terms of religious creed, we must remember that in the Middle Ages the theological and evangelical language was the natural mode of public expression.

It was natural that both papacy and secular government became interested in these still modestly dimensioned mass movements, whose rebellious potential against any organized, insitutional form, Church *and* state, was considerable. No wonder that both Church and state engaged in repressive operations against them, since, after all, like anarchistic, nihilistic, and utopian movements of our days, these sects' program was to "blow up" society and establish paradise on earth: abolition of the family as the nodal point of selfishness, hence promiscuity; community of goods and women; the denial of laws, hierarchy, authority; etc. The most radical sects, such as the Cathars, preached the evil of creation, of giving birth, of life, of social institutions, and so on.

Repression was fierce, and in it the secular and ecclesiastical authorities combined forces. Yet the Church was also intent on regaining the stray sheep for the faith, and understood (Pope Innocent III, for example) that only a Church-sponsored, similarly popular movement could accomplish the work of reconversion. When, with papal encouragement, Dominic went to preach among the Cathars (early thirteenth century), he struck even his opponents' imagination by being modestly attired, by his ascetic ways, his affability, his readiness to engage in debate. This was very different from the haughty ecclesiastical lordbishops and the feudal mores of a large part of the clergy. Dominic's attitude reflected the Church's new perception of the role of the masses, as we would say today, in what one may loosely call "political" life.

Not long after the foundation of the Dominican order, St. Thomas (himself a Dominican) elaborated his theory of the state, as we saw above. Let us now examine briefly how he proceeded to incorporate the "popular" element in his theory, thereby completing the best medieval synthesis for Christians, contemporary and for centuries to come. Just as on the practical level the friars acted in their missionary work among the heretics, Thomas, on the theoretical level, reconciled the theocratic and the popular theses. What does it mean: All power comes from God? What does it mean: The secular ruler rules by divine grace? What does it mean: The people are to be consulted? What does it mean: The people's "good life" is what ultimately matters?

The Thomist synthesis stated that even though God created both the individual and the state, he created man as primary cause and the state as a secondary cause. There is in this statement an ingenious reconciliation of the *realism* and the *nominalism* of the famous medieval debate on universals and particulars, because Thomas recognizes the existence of both, only their different degrees of reality. Individuals are the active elements of the state, and they are created free and multiple; but, as we saw above, while they are free to found, and to live in, this or that organized community, they are bound to found, and to live in, a community. In other words, they *cannot not choose* to live in a state. Thus the state too is elevated to the rank of reality, although a secondary reality; a creation of God, but prompted into existence and action by men.

In the concrete terms of the Middle Ages, the king rules by divine grace, but divine will is transfused into his governing function through the people, mediated by the people. This does not exactly conform to the oversimplified formula *Vox populi vox Dei*, for, as we saw, the majority of the people is neither virtuous nor wise. Nor is it, by far, Marsilius's theory of the people's will making the laws, following their natural desires. And it is certainly not the subordination of the ruler to the people's sovereignty. All these theories, though broached by medieval thinkers, are modern products.

What the Thomist reconciliation suggests is that, in the political realm, God works not through primary agents, that is, individuals (democracy), and not through direct intervention (theocracy), but through secondary agents, such as the state. The people give their consent; they do not rule, they act. But these actions are not the causes of the transfer of authority from God to ruler, only the condition of this transfer. Authority does not rest even for a moment with the people. In other words, there is no contract first, then a contractual designation of the ruler. By the fact of sociability, men give up the best part of their political essence in favor of the laws which guarantee the good management of this part—and only this part. Thus there is no contract, since the individual cannot withhold his consent; and the state has not become either totalitarian or tutelary, since the citizen retains a substantial part of his rights to individual pursuits, even, tacitly, to his unvirtuous inclinations. Be it understood: *qua* citizen, not *qua* Christian.[26]

The Thomist reconciliation of the three elements in the controversy, *spiritual, temporal,* and *popular* power, was broken by thinkers of the following century. In fact, we have analyzed Thomas's synthesis against the background of fourteenth-century political thought, thereby committing the sin of anachronism but gaining a useful perspective.

With this, we conclude the examination of ancient and medieval political thought, at the same time pointing out the necessity to see modern political thought in the light of issues and debates of these earlier periods. This obvious and natural continuity will permit us in later chapters to treat politics and the state in a general overview, and to state the Christian position with regard to them.

Chapter 2
Reflections on State and Politics

The Thomist synthesis may be regarded as a kind of summit of formal political thought, after which, and to the present day, a decline has followed. This does not mean, however, that this synthesis is like a pattern, simply to be applied to political problems as they present themselves. It is implicit in Thomism generally that it gives guidelines for thought and action, but that its framework must be filled with the particular content as situations arise out of possible varieties.

Indeed, the new issues at the end of the Middle Ages and the dawn of modern times changed even in their formulation, To be kept in mind above all is the decrease of religious faith, the various splits in the *christiana respublica,* and the sharp increase of secular-profane thought, attributable to a number of factors: Averroism in the universities (roughly, a divergence of faith and reason), the laicization of town life, the rise of national feeling, the discovery of other continents and populations, living according to non-Western communal structures, the gradual insufficiency of the Aristotelian system (mainly division of the universe into supra- and sublunar parts, now contradicted by astronomy), and so on. Also, the factors that now participated in political life grew in number, beyond pope, emperor, feudal lords, burghers, and populace, and as a result, political power became distributed in a novel way.

In general, the new problem was not how to understand the profane world, the mundane sphere, in reference to the immutable and providential realm of the divine, but how to understand and organize this world without an outside reference, as something autonomous, self-sufficient, self-explanatory. However, let us be careful saying this. The first thing to keep in mind is that the Renaissance was not chiefly a movement toward enlightenment but, in proportion as the Christian worldview was overtaken by others, the Renaissance became a search for an alternative. We saw that the political alternative in the Middle Ages was pagan Rome; an alternative cosmic vision was now engendered by the rediscovered esoteric view, with such ingredients as hermetism, astrology, branches of occult learning, the Kabbala, alchemy, etc. None of these, nor their sum total, amounted to a scientific worldview, but they were immensely popular nevertheless. Thus the process of replacement of the Christian view was gradual, not really successful and complete until Galileo; even after him, only the Aristotelian science was really forced into the background, not the Christian view proper.

The second thing to consider is that we now know enough of the history of science to declare that scientific worldviews for the most part cannot claim "truth value"; they are new perspectives, obtained by a shift of various factors, previously regarded as incontrovertible expressions of the *real*.[1] This means, perhaps paradoxically, that great world systems do not so much cancel each other out as that, when their eclipse arrives, the supposedly discarded models may reappear in a different garb and with new potentials of incorporation into the next world system.

The new political problematic, at the beginning of the era, was not a general one; it was fragmented according to more local issues, as the Christian worldview itself fragmented into various parts. It is agreed that at the threshold of modern times there stands Machiavelli; it is agreed, that is, if we add that much of what the Italian thinker wrote had been anticipated by John of Paris and Marsilius of Padua. The external aspect of the issue remained the same: how to unite the Italian peninsula without the pope, against the pope, whose concerns, being international, could not be harnessed to national matters only. However, beyond the papacy as a "nationalist" target, Machiavelli aimed at the necessity, as he saw it, of discarding the Christian religion too, or at least reducing it to the status of a private cult. Not merely because it could not be an instrument of Italian unity but because—Marsilius had practically said it already—it was a false view of man, of politics, and of the state.

Human beings, Machiavelli held, are basically afraid of one another, not because each is an evil creature but because each lives a separate existence and therefore has a limited view of the future in an ever changing world. Thus men are basically inclined to follow *power* and the possessor of power. But Christianity denies these things; the morality it teaches creates a false view of the real situation in which men find themselves. Consequently, the state in which men would be more at home (than in the Christian state), not because it would be a good state but because it would be more natural, is one whose religion does not deny or repress or preach against the natural status of men. Only with the help of a "natural religion" can one formulate an empirical morality that is suitable for governing and stabilizing the state.

Leo Strauss, in his study of Machiavelli, speaks of the latter's "lowering of the standards," his abandoning of classical virtue, and his attempted conquest of chance in the scheme of things.[2] By lowering man's political vision, Machiavelli suggests, the citizen will be better controlled (for the benefit of each) through centralized institutions; that is, by the exclusion of the one institution—the Church—which represents and teaches an ethical dualism, a divided political loyalty. The ruler—Machiavelli's Prince—is non-Christian; he chooses his "religion" as the one that seems most suitable for his people and for his governance of them, without reference to anything transcendent but only to a "national" creed, an immanent myth.

The medieval model had thus been grossly changed at Machiavelli's hands. Not only was the secular ruler now rid of his ecclesiastical "supervisor," he no longer ruled by divine grace and no longer had to worry about the mediation of power by the people. His main concern was to formulate the right ideology so as to perpetuate and stabilize the regime, in which the choices of the free soul had no longer any place, since everything happened according to a political calculus. Once again, this was not politics, it was ideology.

In actual practice, things were of course not quite that way; they did not accurately follow the model, as in fact they hardly ever do. Yet a new orientation was definitely taken, partly under the impulse of the new, *natural-law* theorists, partly, and benefiting by natural-law doctrines, by the new *political science,* whose chief representatives were Machiavelli and Hobbes. After them, theories of politics and state were never the same again except in isolated instances, when, for example, Thomist thought was rehabilitated or the classical political theories were renewed.[3]

The German scholar, Otto Gierke, notes that the theories on the *dualism* of ruler and pope, abounding in the Middle Ages, contradicted, and thus were ignored by, the modern "*unitary* tendency" manifest in the Western state. The new theorists meant to obliterate the old antithesis and develop the concept of the state's single personality.[4] The still somewhat clandestine Machiavelli was, of course, *par excellence* a representative of the emerging "unitary state." But before and after him, the theorists of the natural law were working in the same direction, in the belief that political matters would thus be simplified and put on a more scientific basis. In this sense, natural law came to represent an apparent return to pre-Christian times, claiming Aristotle and the Stoics, but also the first Christian thinkers, as its founders.

Natural-law theorists were preoccupied with the advisability of discarding the many institutional accretions which throughout medieval times were supposed to obstruct the pure manifestations of governing power: the many corporations, chartered grants, privileges, feudal rights, Church monopolies, family and personal statutes. By abolishing such "intermediate bodies," which in their estimation proliferated in an exaggerated manner, natural-law theorists wanted to strengthen the *royal power* as well as the status of *individuals*, the two concrete elements of society they recognized as basic. Again we may quote Gierke:

> Every relation: community versus individual, ruler versus people was left to Natural Law, sitting enthroned above the whole historically established law.... The natural law theorists agreed in making a definite break with the political ideas originated in the Middle Ages.[5]

Jean Bodin, the French thinker and friend of Henri IV, rejected a limited and divided *majestas*, so that the ruler as a personality absorbed the whole conception of the state; the ecclesiastical theorists, Molina and Suarez, insisted that the social whole have control over its parts, etc. The political order, according to this view, did not require the whole array of corporate bodies created by historical forces and power play during the Middle Ages. Although the Church-advocated "principle of subsidiarity" was at stake, such bodies were deemed to be "Gothic," in the later meaning of the term, that is, too complex and random. The rising spirit of engineering—to simplify and rationalize—so obvious in the contemporary philosophical systems of Descartes and Spinoza, had also penetrated the area of political thought.

Historically, one can justify the work of the simplifiers. They were emerging from a chaotic age, from the deep split in Christendom and consequent civil wars in almost all nations of Europe. Those moderate men, who wanted to put an end to anarchy and devastation, naturally favored a strongly centralized power, unhindered by local rights and privileges of various sorts, such as gave rise to the feudal revolt in France as late as the middle of the seventeenth century, during the childhood of Louis XIV. The end of the process, the final victory of the natural law, came with the Enlightenment. Over the concept of law as it had evolved *organically* during the Middle Ages, the natural law (Gierke calls it the "ideal law," that is, one elaborated abstractly by legal theorists) came to be preferred. In its name the destruction of corporations was completed: in France, by the Revolution which decreed that a Frenchman has only one allegiance, the nation; in Germany, by the bureaucracy of Prussia; and in the Austrian Empire by the reforms of the philosopher-emperor, Joseph II. Only two forces, remarks Gierke, remained facing each other—and, after the philosophical honeymoon, faced each other with increasing bitterness—"the State with its passion for omnipotence, and the Individual with his desire for liberation."[6]

This is the brief story of the impact of natural law. Let us take a glance backward, at Hobbes, heir to the Machiavellian construct, in order to grasp the contribution of the "new political science," as we may call it with hardly any anachronism.

Hobbes is not only an heir of Machiavelli, he is also in the line of the nominalist thinkers, therefore of Ockham. This means that, philosophically, he recognized only the reality of "singulars" or, in the political discourse, individuals. "Outside of us, human beings," he writes, "there is nothing in the world except motions which produce appearances."[7] The human being is also nothing but a mechanism, responding with certain reactions to given stimuli. But this implies no loss in the apprehension of a richly varied universe, because outside us nothing is the way it appears to us, physically or morally. We have a "momentary sentiment" (or sensation) of external reality, but it is subjective, ephemeral, unsure. Words which describe things are highly volatile; they mean this or that according to habit. "Pleasure, love, appetite, desire are words we use to designate the same thing variously envisaged."[8] It follows from these fragile foundations that religious faith, etc., are also only subjective feelings, supported by custom.

Hobbes, like Ockham before and David Hume after him, drew from this extreme skepticism/relativism a politically extreme conservatism. This is logical. If there is nothing we know with any kind of certitude, and if between our subjectivity and a supposed outside world there are no reliable ties, then it follows that, when we raise questions about our political destiny, the best thing is to accept the given situation and not change it. Hobbesian prudence consists of security against upsets, an objective that can be obtained when each individual submits to the king, that is, to the only man who possesses the power to secure peace among his unruly subjects. The selection of the king is done by contract (since only individuals exist, they preexist the state), the consequence of which is the complete alienation of *political* freedom of choice to the Strong Man—to such an extent that, since the ruler commands the citizens' absolute loyalty, he is also empowered to demand absolute spiritual loyalty. Christ's kingdom, Hobbes adds with obvious bad faith, does not belong to this world anyway, at least not until the Second Coming. Hobbes's "religion" is thus indistinguishable from Marsilius's or Machiavelli's "civil religion"; he is only more consequent (and less subject to persecution) than his predecessors when he calls the state a *deus mortalis*.

Hobbes's system seems like a caricature of the medieval controversy about the divine right of the ruler, mediated by the pope or unmediated and direct. The qualitative loss of spirituality is blatant; if nobody seemed to be scandalized by the theories of Hobbes, as public opinion had been when Machiavelli published *his* writings, this only shows the extent of spiritual loss between the end of the Middle Ages and the seventeenth century. But in the light of our previous discussion of natural-law theories, it must be clear why Hobbes met with acceptance: he concentrated, with incredible crudeness, on safeguarding only two interests, favored also by natural-law theorists: the ruler's and the individual citizen's. The ruler's interest, because he had reached the most exalted position, uniting in his person and office the sacred and the profane power; the individual's interest, because Hobbes insisted that there is only one domain where the citizen is free (in fact, this is why the citizen entered the social contract in the first place): the domain of economic transactions.

This is the theoretical starting point, at which three main trends meet:

a) The trend toward the unitary state,
b) The natural-law theories, and
c) The just-born liberal concept of "each man for himself."

For such a combination to become possible, it is clear that the medieval way of positing the problem had to be liquidated. The road was now cleared for

1) The expansion of liberal theories, based "only on individual human beings, each actuated by his private interests," and

2) The imminent conflict between this "sandheap of separate existences"[9] and the state, immensely powerful yet essentially fragile.

True, an equilibrium of powers seemed to have been reached. The medieval corporations and intermediate bodies were cleared out of the way.[10] They were seen as products of anarchical conditions and fruits of unearned privileges, as obstructive monopolies and unnecessary safeguards. Or rather, it was thought that if such safeguards and obstructions were needed in the dark ages of insecurity and fear, they surely could be discarded now, since in the new, enlightened conditions, under the reign of reason, people could easily agree on the reciprocity of their interests. No wonder that the erstwhile pessimism of Machiavelli and Hobbes, grown out of the religious and civil war conditions (in England, France, Italy, and Germany), now gave way to the optimism of a Locke and a Rousseau. However, there was no such essential difference between optimism and pessimism, as one might think, since the basic perception of man and politics remained fundamentally the same for the two groups of thinkers, as well as for their respective epigones.

There were of course extremists, like Hobbes, who held that the human being is a mechanism, registering and reacting to external stimuli. But apart from this radical materialism, these political thinkers agreed on the main points: the individual alone matters, he alone exists; the rest is fiction. Nominalism had penetrated since its late-medieval triumph into scientific as well as political thought, and served as a humanist underpinning for the core of the Protestant view: Every man is the sole judge of his conscience. The similarity between a Calvin and a Hobbes is noteworthy: the reformer conceived of government as imposed by a harsh God as punishment for men's sins; the political philosopher conceived of the king as ruling harshly over men who would otherwise endanger one another: *homo homini lupus.* Yet at the same time the underlying theory of contract relationship proved stronger, in the eyes of the new bourgeois thinkers, than the theory of the ruler's absolute power—in proportion as the bourgeoisie emerged as more vigorous in its attacks against all privileged positions than the monarchy.

In the Middle Ages, two kinds of relationships were recognized in this area: between king and subjects and among the subjects themselves, both relationships standing under God and to be guided by divine doctrine. In modern times, only lip service is paid to God in matters political, and of the two relationships, the one that links the citizens *qua* individuals proved stronger and more important. In French Huguenot circles, then in England, the view became popular that all government and jurisdiction of man over man is artificial, and that the king is a mere servant of the people (Rutherford's *Lex Rex*). In 1648, the tract *Light Shining in Buckinghamshire* declared that, by the grant of God, all are alike free; no individual is intended to rule over his fellow men. The same ideas had been proposed at various times during the Middle Ages, but a powerful Church had been able to "marginalize" these ideas and the civil authority had taken it upon itself to suppress their propagators. Meanwhile both institutions became weaker, while the subtle transformation in the minds of men gradually lifted the people, as the source of sovereignty, to the place of God.

In anticipation of our conclusion of the pre-1789 period, we can do no better in this respect than quote a rather bold passage by a noted English author, who summarized the sequence of ideas of the Huguenots (via the English scene) on the French Revolution: The French political thinkers of the eighteenth century in

> studying Locke, were studying Locke's teachers; and when it is remembered that there is little in Rousseau that was not in Locke, and little in Locke that he did not find in the thinkers of the [Cromwellian] Inter-regnum, the connection of the French Revolution with the [Huguenot thought] becomes apparent.[11]

The prevailing impression among contemporary students of politics is that, in proportion as Western political thought got further away from medieval "obscurantism," the terms in which the issues were framed became more concrete and rational. This impression is hard to sustain. There was a quality in earlier realism which was based on two firm foundations. The first was the historical-traditional-organic development in the life of societies, a development with which people at all times interfered, since such is the natural thing for man to do, but which they also respected, even while modifying it. The second foundation was the favor in which firmly elaborated theories were held, so that political propositions became rooted in a precisely formulated philosophical substratum. The *christiana respublica* also meant a common universe of discourse whose modifications were couched in accepted, habitual terms. Even much later, in the eighteenth century, with its revolutionary innovations, political *realism* about universals had a distinct effect: political language used expressions in such a way that writer, speaker, and public understood one and the same thing by them, considering the terms as having a definite significance. When political writers, up to the beginning of the nineteenth century, used words like "state," "sovereignty," "law," "society," "rights," "constitution," "popular assembly," "estate," "privilege," "equality," "monarchy," "republic," etc., one senses in the writers' minds a respect for these concepts, due to existing and solid realities. The latter can be defined and defended, or overthrown and transformed, yet political institutions retain in the writings of most authors an integrity without which, whatever their value, language about them fast becomes meaningless.[12]

It is hard to decide with precision when the change took place, but probably at the time of romantic effervescence. But already Rousseau, in a principal passage of *Social Contract,* had penned this sentence:

> Each, while giving himself to all, gives himself to none, he is subject to the whole, but not subject to any man, there is no man above him. At the moment when the [social] pact is born, each becomes so completely absorbed in the common Self [*Moi*] which he willed [into existence] that by obeying it, he only obeys himself.

The two sentences are impressively eloquent in the French text, yet all sorts of heterogeneous elements are thrown together in them. Worse, the text has nothing to do with political *reality;* it reads like a number of *subjective* and vague aspirations, projected onto the network of *objective* relationships. The main effect of such writings and the ideas they convey has been far reaching. Modern political thought, in many of its manifestations, does not serve as an escort to reality, taking reality's data in order to draw conclusions about the nature of political man, institutions, the organization of society, and so on. Rather, political science

a) Sets up a number of abstract premises about how man would act *if* he had such and such characteristics (proposed as ideal);

b) Condemns the present situation in the name of these imaginary criteria; and

c) Proposes a utopian construct as the best "political" configuration to follow.

In the case of Rousseau, as in the case of his near contemporaries, Kant and Fichte, individualism and subjectivism achieved a still more advanced penetration into political thought. Since Machiavelli, the difference with the predecessors was that Hobbesian pessimism about man's fate turned into its opposite, but this optimism was equally far from a serene, steady outlook on human affairs and a realistic appraisal of how man may transform the political structure. Again, a text of Rousseau gives the tone:

> I aspire to the moment when, freed from bodily impediments, I shall become my own self, without contradictions, without [inner] division, and will need nothing but my Self [*Moi*] in order to be happy"[13]

It is evident that Rousseau does not have life and death and beatitude in mind, but a vague sentiment of mixed solitude and egolatry. At any rate, his expressed ambition is both antipedagogical (the passage is from *Emile*) and antipolitical, although the author proposed to set down the first principles of a good education and has been known as one of the greatest writers on politics in modern times.

What became of politics and the state in the writings of Rousseau and the German idealists? One way of putting it is that abstract notions, culled from a certain philosophy and a certain literature, were substituted for political concepts. Philosophico-literary notions appeared as speaking for and about man better than religion and politics, as having a kind of exclusive and exalted calling to bring out the *ideal man* from the dross and wretchedness of materiality, superstitions, and political tyranny. In France, the ideal man was called "virtuous," in Germany "cultured," by which latter not so much knowledge as a quality of the soul was meant. Fichte's "ethical will" was a nebulous mixture of self-will and a vague, human-moral essence with which nations (particularly the German nation) were endowed—no longer within the rational structures of a state but as a unique and dynamic mystical core, to be interpreted by the poet and the thinker. The singular quality of the genius, the philosopher-poets Schlegel and Novalis agreed, is to create a world out of nothing, in which the genius would not participate, since he is at all times beyond it, and which he negates with an ironic attitude. Anyway, the only absolute value is not the perfection of the created world, it is the spirit's total freedom.[14]

Excessive individualism and a similarly exaggerated longing for "totality" (of the soul, of the ego's superior pleasures—induced often by drugs—of the nation, of mankind) pushed the prosaic facts of state and political life into the background. Even the French Revolution had its romantics—a St.-Just, for example, or a Robespierre—in whom it is hard to distinguish the parallel aspirations for liberty, despotism, mankind's happiness, and the virtue of government, but also for fierce nationalism, regimentation, the deification of the self. These are not really contradictory ambitions; behind the apparent confusion, their *mélange* expresses an utter subjectivism (*le culte du Moi*), a natural outcome of certain medieval and Renaissance trends of man's self-exaltation.[15] Thus the German romantics viewed the state as a superego (a "Macroanthropos" in Novalis's description) of which individuals are merely incomplete fragments, whereas Rousseau, in his famous essay on inequality among men, extolled the savage as a representative of the world in its youth, and concluded from this metaphor that progress has aimed at the perfection of individuals and the decrepitude of the human species.

Given these premises, the political discourse of the men just mentioned proposes as its objective the abolition of politics, since neither the "great souls" of German idealism nor Rousseau's "noble savage" needed it. Thus we are entitled to label some of the decisive and influential political writings of the age as not really political at all but, rather, a kind of utopian literature with an activist bent. Rousseau's theory, with all its eloquence and seductive style, begins by making a *tabula rasa* of history and human institutions, and follows this devastation of existing reality with the outline of a state's absorption of the citizens' present and future faculty of decision. The earlier-quoted passage about alienation of individual will and its immediate recapture, as transformed into the "general will," is not more than a legalistic fiction. The citizen is completely incorporated in the state; from an anarchic self, supposedly free in the "state of nature," he is metamorphosed into a machine part, just as completely unfree. No wonder that, in order to characterize the theories of Rousseau and his successors, Professor Talmon had to invent an apparently paradoxical but accurate expression, "totalitarian democracy," whereas Tocqueville, in the first half of the nineteenth century not having Talmon's documentation, nevertheless hit upon a similarly telling phrase, "Tutelary State."

Out of the hat into which the political magician had placed only disconnected and free individuals but no preexisting and indispensable institutions which concretely bind them, one cannot take a ready-made and well-functioning society. Rousseau allegedly rebelled against the corrupt society of his time and sought to discipline it by building a strong state which would contain and limit it. Hegel was to blame him for this disregard of the concrete freedoms that are necessary for a healthy civil society; we might add to this criticism that the state that Rousseau proposed was not strong but totalitarian. In other words, at both ends a failure.

But Kant and Fichte did not improve on this model. True, their chief reputation is not that of writers on politics; however, both were philosophers whose line of thought carried them from pure speculation into the area of political thought, if we prolong these lines and append to them further utterances. Both regarded politics as a means to bring into existence a miraculous machine which will satisfy the soul and fill it with admiration, moving it to accomplish wonders. Kant saw humanity as gradually emerging to a state of moral autonomy, until it reaches the stage of a universal republic, consisting of smaller but similarly universalist republics. Since the goal is thus arbitrarily set, Kant does not find it hard to choose arbitrary signposts on the way. Thus the French Revolution, including its most sanguinary, terrorist phases, is approved by Kant as an opening to a radiant future, and he would also have approved the benevolent despotism of the Prussian kings—if they had not insulted him by not listening. History, for Kant, was ultimately to culminate in a universal constitutional order, securing perpetual peace.

Kant's disciple, Fichte, who pushed the former's epistemological subjectivism to new heights by affirming that only the "self" (*Ich*) exists, contradicted himself when he extolled the German nation (that is, an aggregate of selves) to first place in the newly opening world scene. The contradiction is bridged when Fichte endows the German nation with a *national self,* thereby creating a questionable new entity in the place of the medieval empire, Church, estates, and corporations. According to Fichte, the Germans are the primary nation, the others being "resigned to represent only a derivative product."[16] But every nation, he writes, wants to disseminate the good things peculiar to it; it wants to assimilate the entire human race to itself in accord with an urge planted in man by God, an urge on which the community of nations, the frictions among them, and their development toward perfection rest.

We see that Rousseau, Kant, and Fichte (to mention only them) brought forward new entities in the political debate: General Will, Universal Republic, the self-asserting Nation-State, and so on. It is noteworthy that these thinkers cared little for the precise elaboration of their political theories, and the vacuum was filled by their conviction that "historical evolution" (which is not questioned) is on their side—that they describe the future as it emerges from today's magma. Thus we may speak in their case of a *rhetorical* approach to politics, a rhetoric filled emotionally and made eloquent by the belief that the "self" which produced it is in some kind of communion with "history." The prophet and his god are inextricably intertwined; one hardly knows where the thinker's pronouncements end and history begins.[17]

Over against these prophet-thinkers, two other groups deserve mention before we consider the two powerful personalities who gave political thought yet another orientation, Hegel and Marx. The two trends are antirevolutionary thought (Burke, J. de Maistre) and the "liberal" school (Adam Smith, Bentham, J. S. Mill).

The French Revolution had not run its full course when various personalities throughout Europe gave expression to their horror before the atrocities committed by its leaders and partisans. Edmund Burke in England, and later Metternich in Austria, understood the revolutionary behavior as not merely and randomly producing regrettable excesses but as following from the nature of the ideology which had watered the whole movement that led to the revolution. The debate was similar to the one we witness in our century: Was Stalinism a regrettable excess of the Marxist movement and Soviet state or the natural expression of Marxian ideology? Whatever the merits of the case, the "conservative movement" all over Europe first defined itself in reaction to the French Revolution; it called itself "counter-revolutionary," while its opponents tagged it "reactionary."

Burke's mild skepticism was a sufficient expression of most Englishmen's revulsion as the news daily reached the British Isles from France. Joseph de Maistre was nearer and more involved (he was for a long time a Freemason); he wanted to go to the roots of what he perceived as not the case of France only but a Europe-wide phenomenon. In elaborating a counterdoctrine to the revolutionary one, Maistre first attacked the blind optimism of Rousseau, his abstract treatment of man in general, the original virtue of the "good savage," the subsequent corruption "by society." Maistre's arguments, while not as profound and especially not as balanced as his partisans have claimed to this day,[18] amount to a good criticism immediately after the revolutionary events. When working out the counterrevolutionary case, it is impossible that one not take account of these arguments.

Maistre shows primitive man as a receptacle of crude instincts, criminal behavior, and animal appetites. In the light of modern anthropology and ethnography, he is as wrong as Rousseau and Hobbes, since both thinkers, and Maistre after them, idealized archaic man in one way or another so that he should fit their respective positions. But Maistre's position may be preferred because, while he overdrew his picture of the "savage,"[19] he could thus demonstrate that not society, but man is the source of corruption, in primitive as well as developed times. This position explains why Maistre was a firm believer in original sin, and consequently in the necessity of surrounding the individual with safeguards against his own evil drives. Again, the trouble is that Maistre tends to dramatize the evil in man, just as Rousseau underplays it. Hobbes comes to mind as one who would have been an opponent to Maistre, as the latter describes what situation would prevail in society and the body politic if very strong institutions did not watch over the citizen from the cradle to the grave. "The child's cradle must be surrounded with dogmas; when his reason awakens he should find all his opinions already formed, at least those which direct his behavior. There is nothing more important for him than his prejudices" (*Studies on Sovereignty*). This is the anti-Rousseau position, in pedagogy and society, that Edmund Burke also would have accepted.

Yet Maistre goes too far when he derives his concept of the state from his initial perception of the effect of original sin. He sets morality, government, and religion on *prejudice* as the foundation, as if people were moral, religious, and civic minded not because they comprehend the good of these things but because of attitudes that are inculcated in them at a tender age. This is a case of circular reasoning, since at one point the inculcator of opinions and prejudices must have been himself convinced, due to his reasoning capacity, of the goodness of what he teaches. Maistre, however, pays no attention to the quicksand on which he has stepped and goes on practically to agree with Machiavelli and Hobbes:

> There must be a State-religion as there must be a State-politics; or rather, the religious and political dogmas must be so combined and fused as to form together a general or *national reason*, strong enough to repress the aberrations of individual reason [*Studies on Sovereignty*].

As a result of this almost fatalistic conception of evil in man, the Maistrean state is rigid and pitiless, with sovereignty placed nominally in God and the ruler, but really in the hands of the public executioner, on whom "rest all greatness, all power, all subordination."[20] The executioner is, of course, a symbol; he stands for social cohesion, functioning institutions, civic discipline, continuity. Likewise, Maistre sees not the ruler (he saw that a king of France could be demoted, imprisoned, and executed) but the pope, the Church, and its dogmas and structure as the guarantee of the body politic. But again, we see a vast exaggeration whose basis in man's "evil nature" repels us as much as Rousseau's state, based on "man's goodness." And Maistre's *elogium* of the public executioner strikes us, in this age of an omnipotent KGB within an omnipotent Soviet system, as ominous, a prefiguration of horrors he did not imagine.

What we call "liberal" political thought (taking for granted its wisdom) is not recognized by all as "political" thought. It resembles, in fact, the other ideologies, inasmuch as liberalism also regards the state as something close to an evil concentration of power, to be at all times watched and, if possible, reduced to what has been called a "minimal state." If it is not completely condemned, the reason for tolerating it may be historical rather than rational. The bourgeoisie, whose ideology liberalism is, was as strong in the eighteenth and nineteenth centuries as feudalism or the absolute monarchy was earlier; thus it was able, like the other systems, to make use of the state for the promotion of its own interests. The state was understood by liberals as a loose and flexible framework, securing orderly, mostly economic transactions, building the required infrastructure for such transactions, and maintaining peaceful conditions, including the legislation necessary for the pursuit of economic progress. A large part of foreign policy was devoted to the expansionist interests of the domestic market, thus covering the planet with liberal assumptions—but also giving rise to a reaction which has exploded in our century.

The heart of the liberal system is freedom from obstructions to trade, then freedom from the state, too, which clears away these obstructions. The enormous popularity of liberalism is mostly due to three factors.

The first is the theory that for the system to function well, it must establish a climate of general freedom and exchange, not merely in the economic area but also in the world of intellectual endeavors and culture.[21] The big entrepreneur, even if his earlier activities earned him the label "robber baron" or, more mildly, "captain of industry," often turned maecenas, filling the role always held in the domain of art, architecture, and science by the powerful, whether Roman emperors, feudal lords, Renaissance popes, or great monarchs. This role secured for the entrepreneurial side of liberalism the understanding, often the servility, of the intellectual milieus, at a time when these milieus emerged as increasingly influential through the mass-circulation press, popularized scientific writings, and universal compulsory education. The public, open to persuasion by the class of intellectuals, also became a sympathetic audience of the spokesmen for the liberal system.

The second influencing factor toward the wide acceptance of liberalism was its release of energies in a great many directions. The economic practice it sponsored was designed to satisfy the productive capacities of one group and the absorbing (consuming) capacities of other groups, so that wherever liberalism and, with it, the inseparable capitalist practices penetrated, they brought into existence entire classes of people who in a relatively short time were catapulted to a high living standard and positions of political pressure, if not indeed political power. Not only capitalism accompanied the liberal penetration;[22] democracy was also in the escorting group, with the result that Europe- and America-based liberals (entrepreneurs and idea men) soon had like-minded and symmetrical classes of liberals in every part of the planet, from Argentina to India. Press power and school power were thus every year multiplied, and with them the amplitude of the worldwide echo that liberals were able to generate around their issues, interests, and personalities.

The third factor was the belief, spread by the tremendous power of the press, of the school system (but also by "high culture") that liberalism is a point of arrival for mankind, the summit of progress toward which history had been advancing. Naturally, every system that has conquering ambitions creates for itself a flattering image of history, but in the case of liberalism (as suggested before) the agents of the worldview had the kind of unlimited means of propaganda at their disposal that the Church had had in its most powerful days, the centuries from Charlemagne to the Renaissance. A wide variety of philosophical groups found themselves helped by the recruitment made possible by liberal tolerance; first of all the liberal groups themselves, for whom tolerance itself—open-mindedness, open society, pluralism of belief, etc.—was the apparent content of their ideology. It was not easy or popular to point at tolerance as not so tolerant after all, since it meant the condemnation of all systems of thought that could be designated "intolerant," whether religion, the protest against economic and cultural practices, or the philosophical critique of the liberal premises. Thus liberalism, like systems of thought that ride the crest of the waves at any time, was taken to be the "natural" way of thinking, since it brought with it, in Bentham's words, the greatest happiness to the largest mass—in the words of Adam Smith, the greatest amount of merchandise for the waiting consumers, or for J. S. Mill, the best way to secure everybody's rights, limited only by the other fellow's similar rights.

These were heady words and respectable achievements. They covered, quite successfully for a while, the voices of warning and criticism. One of the earliest representatives of liberal concepts in politics, Montesquieu, warned that the more people want to profit by their freedom, the nearer the time when they will lose it altogether. "At first, many little tyrants rise, then soon a single one. The people lose everything, including the advantages of their corruption."[23] Montesquieu's remark, a truism ever since Plato, casts light on the permanent controversy around the notion of the sovereignty of the people, to which thoughtful men

never consented, or, if they did, with the proviso that it be exercised in name only or be surrounded with all kinds of limitations.
Montesquieu wrote that the only occasion for the populace to
participate in the affairs of government is when it elects those
who will represent it. The people, as such, are incapable of
executing resolutions.[24]

In a liberal regime, all sorts of contradictions arise, though
they are masked for a long time by the possibilities that
liberalism offers to individual energy and to a nation's expansionist spirit. We have located the source of the main contradiction: the liberal assumption that society may be so tolerant as to
be neutral, a marketplace where all ideas can be freely and indefinitely exchanged. This model is copied from the neutrality
of the exchange of material goods, where the common de-
nominator is material interests expressed in money. But such a
neutrality

a) Could not exist in the domain of ideas, which involves beliefs, convictions, passions, loyalties, arguments, and

b) Is false because it hides an ideology, with its presuppositions
and consequences.

Walter Lippmann was wrong when he wrote that "all that the
defenders of freedom have to defend in common is a public
neutrality and a public agnosticism."[25] Lippmann himself gives
the lie to his statement when he writes (sixty-five pages further):
"If the philosophers teach that religious experience is a purely
psychological phenomenon, related to nothing beyond each
man's psychic condition, then they will give educated men a bad
intellectual conscience if they have religious experiences" (p.
178).

The illustration is quite telling, even if it is not readily put in
the correct framework. Liberalism has indeed a strong inclina-
tion toward "public agnosticism," because it cannot deny its origins: opposition to state and Church and their strongly held
beliefs. Thus authorities and public figures, under a liberal re-

gime, tend to favor and appoint professors of philosophy (to remain with Lippmann's example) who indeed teach that religious experience has nothing to do with reason, and that it is a subjective (emotional or psychic) phenomenon. Those who appoint such professors do so because of their commitment to the agnostic worldview; also, book and magazine publishers tend to favor them, and the press will give wider coverage to their views than to those of their opponents. Finally, the school child, at the farthest receiving end of the process, will be taught that the views of the philosophy professor in question are absolute truths—although, according to the "public philosophy," which is agnostic, all truths are relative—except, of course, this one!

It is therefore important to understand that liberalism

a) Copies the market relationships in its efforts to make sense of all other relationships, and

b) Professes the "economic man's" neutrality while imposing on society a basically intolerant, though well camouflaged, worldview.

Yet it cannot comprehend its own fallacy because the worldview it professes does not recognize anything above the individual, except "culture" and "values," which are nothing but expressions of individual tastes and preferences. It is true, of course, and we discussed it apropos of the Thomist concept of the ruler's authority, that "in the order of being, the individual persons, as the only substantial rational beings, are first."[26] Nevertheless, the state as a secondary agent is also in the divine plan, as well as other intermediate communities, all promoting man's happiness. To speak of a "minimal state" is not to grasp the reality of the common good; it is to reduce it to Bentham's quantified formula or to Smith's "invisible hand" which is supposed to harmonize all interests, provided everybody pursues his own selfish ends.

The reality and significance of the common good, and of the state which represents it, can be illustrated by an example on which liberals and Christians are on opposite sides. Take the presently burning issues of pornography, teen-age contraception, drug addiction, and abortion. The liberal argues that all these things ought to be legalized, first, because if they are not, the users simply resort to clandestine, and harmful, ways of obtaining them; second, because if there are enough consumers for certain goods and services, no law should prevent such transactions in the open market. Indeed, according to its premises, liberal reasoning cannot go beyond this position without violating these premises: the law of quantitative satisfaction and the law of supply and demand.

The Christian argument, on the other hand, is based, first, on the concept of society as divinely ordained, thus directed to morality, and second, on the concept of the community as a coherent whole, a corporation, whose integrity and moral well-being should not be fragmented. Society and state, in the Christian concept, cannot countenance the open practice of pornography, etc., by a part of the population, because, though in a nonascertainable and noncalculable way, this would affect the common consciousness, thus the conscience of all. This *corporate sense* is a crucial tenet of Catholic teaching, before which the liberal remains uncomprehending or even hostile, accusing it of signifying conformism, authoritarianism, and thought control. Yet the "corporate sense" is just another way of designating the "common good."[27]

In light of these considerations, it is easy to agree with some contemporary Christian critics of the liberal state and society. "The liberal society," writes E. J. Hughes,

> had been erected on grounds from which men had exiled the conception of society as a *communitas communitatum* with its insistence on the attachment to social organization of a transcendent moral purpose, its functional unity of individuals and classes, its estab-

lished dominion of ethics over economics. It had replaced this with a society conceived as a joint-stock
company . . . a society in which the State was a matter
of convenience . . . and man . . . through the resolute
and relentless material accumulation, the Economic
Man.[28]

One can say, generally, that the critics of liberal ideology make
these two, related points: liberal ideology has built liberal society
and its residual state on the weakest political entity, individual
man, and, furthermore, has focused on man's ethically weakest
aspect, his economic interests. This doubly fragile illusion could
indeed be upheld in the early period of liberal capitalism. As
Rommen writes, "the Calvinist was able to demand a minimal
State because, as a pious believer in Scripture as rule of life, he
was able to organize his social life better than a government."[29]
This was still only capitalism, not yet combined with liberal
ideology; but Scripture did not remain long the axis of Western
credal thought. Liberalism substituted for it a series of new
axioms from which generally agnostic, so-called humanistic objectives were derived.[30] The consequence was "a doctrine of man
which dispenses with man's relation to the Eternal God" and
thus "fails to do justice to the double element in the human
being, the foundation of the christian doctrine: freedom and
creatureliness."[31] This is why the individual is made the highest
judge of truth and the final arbiter of all social issues. Through
the legalism that this stance entails, society accords its enemies
the power to destroy it, and the state submits to this power,
rooted in the contract theory. Surveying the liberal Western
societies, Alexander Solzhenitsyn summed up this neglected aspect of our ills in his speech at Harvard University in June 1978:

I have spent all my life under a communist regime,
and I will tell you that a society without any objective
legal scale is a terrible one, indeed. But a society with

> no other scale but the legal one, is not quite worthy of
> man either. . . . Whenever the tissue of life is woven of
> legalistic relations, there is an atmosphere of moral
> mediocrity, paralyzing man's noblest impulses.

The assumption of this passage is that no scale of values, except the legal one, has remained in liberal society. Patriotism, spiritual insight, the claims of right morality, the admonitions of religion, the sense of the common good—all have been flattened in the name of "inalienable individual rights," woven into exclusively legal relationships. This passage in Rommen's work sums it up: "The ideal of an individualist and liberalist society becomes the depreciation and minimizing of the State, and the exaltation of the laissez-faire philosophy which implies the total subjection of the sovereign power to the rules of commutative justice." The logical outcome is a "society without the State, without politics, sovereign will or autonomous common good, without authority or government."[32]

There is a theory, particularly popular in progressivist ecclesiastical circles, that *socialism,* including its virulent, Marxist variety, is a punishment wrought by God on liberal society for its sins: exploitation of man by man, disregard for communitarian principles, the atomization of society into uncaring, selfish individuals. The Russian writer, Nicholas Berdyaev, an Orthodox converted to Catholicism, indicted not just liberalism, but "Christian society," as a culprit that has failed to live the truth it carries in its heart. By not following Christ's teaching, Western society, especially in its latest, liberal capitalist phase, became a traitor to the Lord. Socialism, although a harsh system too, is destined to play Attila to a corrupt segment of mankind.

This is, of course, an idealized, romantic view of socialism-Marxism, based, moreover, on a substantial error. Even Maritain, in his middle and later years, subscribed to this erroneous view, which reads something like the following. As a political philosophy, liberalism ignores, for the benefit of man in the abstract, all the heavy burdens that lie on man in real life. The absolute right of each part to realize its choice tends to dissolve the whole in anarchy and to make impossible any realization of freedom or any achievement of autonomy within the order and through the instrumentality of social life.[33]

Thus far Maritain, the Thomist, is correct. It is in the nature of things that we surrender our temporal goods, and if necessary our lives, for the welfare of the community, and that social life impose on each individual, as part of the whole, many restraints and sacrifices. This was the message of Moses and Pericles, of Aristotle and St. Thomas. The question is, however, did socialism, in theory and practice, remedy the shortcomings of liberalism? Did it not exacerbate the latter's ills by allowing a *part* (a political party) to take over the whole of society and the state, subject them to its own interests, and encourage by its inefficiency and dishonesty the very selfishness (stealing state property, corruption at all levels, the emergence of a greedy and imperious "new class," a brutal clinging to power) it was supposed to abolish? In the process of bringing about the "classless society," socialism, even when it has repudiated Marx, has leveled the social landscape, favored the mediocre, and disadvantaged original minds and endeavors. And we do not even mention the monstrous acts by which communism surpasses the horrors of Assyria and the cruelties of Ivan the Terrible.

The theory of socialism as a "chastisement" for the sins of the liberal West does not hold water, except in the innocuous sense that, in the succession of world systems, the subsequent event reacts in many, often haphazard ways to what has preceded it. It is more true to say, simply, that discontent with the practices of early capitalism gave rise to the critique of economic and social injustices. A concrete example is the suppression of corporations by one of the earliest decrees of the French Revolution

(November 1789), so that the subsequent complaints by workers showed the aspiration of restoring these corporations in some new way, through the workers' unions and their syndicalist movement.

It is also true that, as the German historian Troeltsch said in a famous address, "Natural Law and Humanity" (October 1922), German romanticism engendered a metaphysical—mystic vision of individuality as meaning the embodiment assumed from time to time by the Divine Spirit, whether in persons or in some superpersonal organization of collective life. This vision brought forth, on one hand, the specifically German idea of community and state, from Adam Müller to Ferdinand Tönnies, and on the other hand the spectacular political philosophy of Hegel and Marx.

The above notations were not meant to exhaust the motives which produced the Hegelian theory of the state. Hegel himself, an extremely complex philosophical personality, recognized his link to various sources, to Plotinus, to Spinoza, to the medieval mystic Meister Eckhart, and so on. Suffice it to say that, in his own mind and in that of his immediate and distant followers to this day, Hegel is the master thinker who turned philosophy into a "science" and solved the "riddle of history." In his own right and as Marx's chief inspiration, he deserves to be carefully studied. His political theory is the last grandiose system which left a durable imprint on Western thought; it is also a substantive challenger of Catholic concepts in this area.

The core of Hegelian thinking is the proposition that what is incomplete, what does not fill out its essence, *is not;* therefore it strives to become complete through the "dialectical" movement. Insofar as morality has always been an individual, subjective matter, it *is not,* whether it is the morality taught by Socrates, Christ, or Kant. Hegel sets out to locate objective morality and finds it embodied in rights, duties, and laws—that is, in publicly recognized entities that have public, historical, and philosophical significance. Objective morality is thus given concrete embodiment, according to Hegel, in family, in civil society, and above all in the state. It is in the state that man finds his ultimate meaning, because the state is the actual reality of the "ethical idea," the most sublime and rational embodiment of the "world spirit."

In family and civil society, the "ethical idea" is merely lived, but remains quasi unconscious and powerless. In the state, however, it is revealed as *thought,* as a universal object, as the primary manifestation of the divine. In consequence, religion is only a private matter, expressing the individual's faith at a rudimentary level, the level of images and feelings. In a conflict between religion and the state, decision belongs to the latter because through the state, in the state, religion is understood as thought and reason: it becomes truly conscious of itself. It is for the state to actualize the content of religion, which religion expresses only imperfectly through its own means.

From this it follows that religion, as taught by the Church (Hegel's most bitter criticism was directed at the Catholic Church), is the Hegelian state's main adversary because Catholic teaching separates the sacred and the profane, thus preventing the state, locked up in the profane sphere ("secular rule," in medieval language), from self-realization as total reason. In contrast, Hegel praised Protestantism, where state, religion, and philosophy coincide, helping the Spirit and the real (subject and object) to be reconciled. The state is "church" and "philosophy" at the same time. As Hegel's sagacious commentator, Eric Weil, notes:

> No compromise is possible between Catholic transcendence and the modern [Hegelian] State. The State is modern in proportion as it brings about that which religion opposes to this-worldly life as a kingdom not of this world.[34]

A very clear statement indeed, not merely about the Hegelian conception but also about the state and its policies as the Western world has known them in the last two hundred years. During this period the state has vacillated between the liberal-contractual theory, which weakens it to the point of near abolition, and the Hegelian-socialist theory, which holds that the state must assume as its essential task the shouldering of all the aspirations of its citizens, including the spiritual aspirations, duly absorbed, of course, and organized as a "state spirituality."

Needless to say, both ways of thinking are contrary to the Catholic understanding of the state, but the Hegelian theory displays the additional defect of suppressing, implicitly and at once, man's dual membership in the spiritual and the secular realms. Naturally, Hegel takes it for granted that the essence of the state is the very law of reason, so that every human being who is endowed with rationality must find in the state the representative of his rational will. It is evident, however, that the citizen of the Hegelian state is thus less than rational; at best, he resembles the citizen of Aristotle's *polis,* whose ethical dimension is a kind of state-integrated moral behavior. Aristotle is excusable for not seeing beyond the *polis;* Hegel, on the other hand, stands under the charge of monstrous arrogance for integrating the transcendental aspiration into his rational state.

The same is true with regard to freedom. In the Hegelian perspective, freedom on the individual's level is a mere formless aspiration, exercised for the benefit of self, family, and transactional interests; it is almost the spontaneous arbitrariness of the animal. Only about the state can one declare that it is free or unfree. Only the state is able to originate freedom—more precisely, to incarnate it. Here, then is another philosophical defect of the master thinker, particularly obvious if seen from a Catholic point of view.

The state, for Hegel, is not a secondary agent, a means to serve human nature and its God-directedness. It is, to speak the Scholastic language, a "first cause," the ultimate and most perfect realization of the universal design, the incarnation of the world-spiritual idea.

The Hegelians argue that their master was solely interested in elaborating a scientific concept of the state, the state as it appears in history, the main channel of human activities, which looms very large in political life. He had nothing to do with the citizen's private devotions and subjective representations of what the divinity signifies in his inner life. To this apologia we answer that Hegel and the Hegelians use the term "scientific" in an arbitrary way, excluding or minimizing what they do not regard as essential to the public sphere. Precisely in the public sphere, where the state occupies, legitimately, such a large place, it is necessary that it not be the sole occupier of man's attention and interests, that it share the public sphere with the Church, which occupies another order, just as important as the political order. Not merely because it is prudent for man to have two masters, in which case state and Church would be regarded as political conveniences, products of two contracts, but because human life is inconceivable without spiritual freedom, manifested through positive and institutionalized religion. Otherwise, nothing stops the state, contrary to the Hegelian assumption with its world-spiritual scheme, from becoming totalitarian, a radicalized variety of the Hobbesian state.

There is a notable ambiguity in the discourse of Hegelians. You see, they point out, whatever the theoretical criticisms against the Hegelian state, the modern state *is,* and behaves like the one conceived by the philosopher of Berlin. This is because he abstained from idle speculation about the state in the abstract and scrutinized the laws of historical evolution—the laws of the "world spirit" as it gradually unfolds—and concluded that the modern state was to follow such and such a course. In short, in Hegel's thought the necessary evolution coincides with the nature of things.[35]

This is fallacy. First, because there are standards above both what *is* and what the philosopher finds *best.* These are generally the moral standards, even though Hegel sidesteps them with the argument that for moral standards to be more than "subjective images and sentiments," they must be embodied in the state as the "ethical idea." This is circular reasoning, to which the Hegelians remain unresponsive. The second reason why Hegel's statement about the modern state is fallacious is that, since his day, there has been a variety of states, some conforming to, others contradicting, the master scheme. At any rate, the one that claims to be in the line of direct succession to Hegel's thought is the Marxist state—not exactly a flattering exhibition item.

All in all, the Hegelian state must be judged on its own merits, and in our case from the angle of Catholic teaching. We have said that Hegel's philosophical personality was complex, by which we meant that it mixed (or juxtaposed?) a mystical conception of forces that shape the world and down-to-earth, extremely valuable insights and observations. In Hegel's perspective, the modern state, as a historical product, would display the following features:

a) It would be a strong, constitutional monarchy, served by a centralized and competent administration;

b) Economically, it would be decentralized, because Hegel, in contrast to Rousseau, whom he criticized, held firmly that civil society should be dynamic and free;

c) There would be no state religion as such since, as was said before, the state embodies religion; and

d) In external affairs the state would be absolutely sovereign in its acts. (Hegel criticized Kant for his ideal of a universal republic, limiting the actions of the member republics.)

So far, the Hegelian state is indeed reasonably structured; in fact, it prefigures, beyond the liberal phase, the late-twentieth-century state, which, at least outside the liberal-democratic West and the Communist regimes, tries to combine a strong executive power, served by a bureaucracy, with a relatively free transactional (civil) segment of society. In this respect, Hegel's state resembles nothing better than those of Salazar and Franco. Elections, Hegel wrote, are a capitulation before the vested interests, against whose inordinate power the elections are held in the first place! A sharp insight, which is a far-reaching critique of the democratic-liberal regime.

Yet the other side of the picture that Hegel presents is less encouraging. The state, as the "ethical idea" incarnate, is threatening less because it *is* the state (in any case, a tremendous power concentration) than because it shows Hegel's concept of the "world spirit" as an immanent principle and the universe as a monistic enterprise. No room is left for an extrauniversal moving force; all things are, as in a machine, rationally integrated, thus capable of crushing the human being.

Hegel's philosophy has been called the "philosophy of freedom," by which people meant, however, a "philosophy of the spirit" (*Geistes philosophie*). Yet the spirit which is free has nothing to do with the free spirit. The Hegelian *Geist* is not outside the world and man; it is a blind force which cannot do otherwise than it does and whose idea of itself is not divine knowledge, only a process of self-realization at the end of history. Of the Christian God, Hegel said that it is now time to unmask it as a fiction, as an "alien individual," projected during the time of ignorance by man's subjective imagination into an equally imaginary "outside." Now, in the time of total knowledge, it should be "brought back" and revealed as the working of history, of the state, of human freedom as explicated in history and the state.

Why bring back the "alien individual" *now*? Because Hegel, a sharp observer of concrete events around him (he called the morning newspaper the "modern bible"), was also a falsely mystical thinker, who actually believed his philosophical system was the last, the culmination of what can be said about the world in time and space—that is, history and nature, tied together by his logic. Like other immanentist thinkers—and false mystics—Hegel saw himself as the final product of the evolution of thought, his life coincident with the final maturation of history, with the self-knowledge of the "world spirit." All the defective speculations about God could now be discarded, and God—or rather the energy that the "God idea" always represented but was not properly used—could be harnessed to the service of mankind and revealed as the central process of history.

The philosopher Eric Voegelin called Hegel a "sorcerer," a man who transmutes the working of his mind into the transformations of history. Sorcerer or demiurgos, Hegel thought he inaugurated the last stage of history, the Rule of Reason. In this stage, the philosopher does not merely register and comment on the phenomena, he transforms them and brings about changes in them the way the alchemist changes one metal into another.[36]

Let us bear in mind two dicta, of Engels and Marx. Engels referred to the Hegelian system as the last word in German philosophy, after which only action remains. Marx wrote that philosophy thus far had been content to interpret the world; henceforward it would have the task of changing it.

This sounds like a recognition that the world, in spite of its privileged "Hegelian moment," would continue, filled with action. Indeed, Hegel and Marx were in agreement that events in history are moved by the sentiment of dissatisfaction, and that consciousness does not precede events but registers them, when the action is already engaged. Thus both could consider their thinking as possible only because the objectives that this thought set forth were in the process of termination, or at least maturity. The owl of Minerva, runs a well-known Hegelian formula, takes flight when darkness falls—suggesting that intelligence must accept the modest function of commenting on events as they near their end. In the Hegelian perspective, these reflections would indicate that history is not yet at its terminus, so that mankind will behave as before: politics as usual. New forms of the state will spring up, be fought for, be victorious or defeated.

Yet the entire Marxian enterprise tends to demonstrate that

a) Politics exists only where exploiting and victimized classes are locked in combat;

b) The state and its apparatus is the former's instrument for maintaining itself in power (hence the new slogan among our radicals that the state is "institutionalized violence");

c) The contradictions between bourgeoisie and proletariat must end in a revolutionary confrontation and with the latter's planetwide victory;

d) Once the proletariat is in (dictatorial) power, all classes will be abolished, thus also the class struggle; and

e) The state itself will wither away and the opulent, peaceful society will be installed.

Now this would suggest that, as in Hegel's political philosophy, only for different reasons and following a different course, Marxism too posits an "end of history"; in fact an imminent one, if we are to believe the predictions of Marx, Lenin, Trotsky, and others. If that is the case, politics as we have known it has only a short time before its extinction, because the leveling of all differences and the satisfaction of all needs (the idea, that is, of discontent as the motor force of history) will bring to a halt the political struggle, objectified in the class struggle. Simultaneous with the liquidation of politics will be that of the state, since the classless society will need only rotating administrators, the tasks in such a society being simple (like the four operations of arithmetics, said Lenin), and jealousy, greed, and the desire to hoard for evil times, or the inordinate ambition for more and better, will have become meaningless.

Thus Marx's activism was to be stepped up only for a brief, revolutionary period, after which peace and quiet were to descend on a forever satisfied human race. As Stalin explained, in a fully Communist society the changes—in fact, qualitative leaps in the dialectical movement—no longer occur in a brusque, revolutionary manner, like explosions, and they do not end by the overthrow of the (Communist) regime. The change comes from above, through the regime's initiative and with the support of the "masses of peasants and workers."[37]

The Christian critique, addressed to Marx, is then also the critique addressed to Hegel but aggravated by the special features of Marxism. Some of these features are

   a) The materialist ontology;

   b) Man is the product of nature, to whose materiality he is bound to return;

   c) The design to create a new man, even more harmonious with matter;

   d) The concept of conflict and struggle as the result of class differences;

   e) The determinism of mind, morality, art, and convictions by material conditions and membership in a class; and so on.

These are the philosophical foundations for a political thought which can only be called extremely elementary. As we have seen, politics is implicitly defined in Marxism as the struggle between classes, first for economic advantages, ultimately for the utopian goal of extinguishing the struggle through the dictatorship of one class. This class, the proletariat, is arbitrarily called the "universal class," and it is naively assumed that if everybody will be a member of it, no more envy, discontent, and desire to do better than one's neighbor will arise to disturb the classless landscape. The state is envisaged with no less naiveté. Of all its rich endowments throughout history, Marx focused on one: its mechanism of keeping power in the hands of the possessing strata. But suppose all citizens, or nearly all, become possessors? Marx answers that what matters is the ownership of the means of production—since he could not foresee the day when these things will be publicly owned—yet without the disappearance of classes, indeed with the exacerbation of class differences, as is the case in Communist countries.

Would the state, under these circumstances, still be an instrument of exploitation? There have been varieties of states since the time of Marx, and each case indicates that the state is indispensable for giving shape to society and fulfilling functions that society as such cannot shoulder. Nor does the state show signs of a gradual self-liquidation. In fact, it has grown so ubiquitous in East and West alike that

a) It has assumed the task of sociological and economic manipulation: progressive taxation, determination of national priorities, social and racial integration of schools, neighborhoods, and jobs; and

b) It has acquired intellectual-moral domination over people and issues to such an extent that, from sports to health, from science to industry, from art to education, it is expected to make the final decisions—beyond the ones which belong to it according to its nature.[38]

The "welfare state," while weak in authority and affirmation of sovereignty, is anything but a mechanism in the hands of exploiting classes. It is run by what one may prefer to call "feudal power concentrations" which confuse the neat Marxian landscape, elaborated 140 years ago: government and auxiliary bureaucracies, labor unions, big business, and the media.

The main objection to Marx's idea of politics and state, however, is not in the area where he accumulated errors and ventured wrong prophecies. The main political objection is in the relationship between man and state, or, more exactly, the place of man in the Marxian worldview. The notion of a strong state *per se* is not inimical to Hebrew-Christian thought. The Old Testament abounds in cases where the people ask the king for bread, justice, and leadership. Nor did Christ deny Caesar his due; and we saw in Tertullian that Christians paid more sincere, because divinely ordained, homage to the emperors than the pagans. Nor are Christians surprised by the changes in the fortunes of the state, now weak, then strong. They know there is no progress in this regard: the weak state in the West is paralleled by the strong state elsewhere, and we cannot jubilate that our liberal century has known no Genghis Khan and his hordes, when it has witnessed Stalin, Mao Tse-tung, and the genocide inflicted on their own people by Cambodian's leaders, crazed by ideology.

The reason why popes called communism "intrinsically perverse" lies elsewhere, namely, in its thesis that the human being is a part of material nature and hence is entirely determined by material circumstances, the organization of which depends on an elite's claiming perfect knowledge of history and therefore complete command of the people. It is of little importance that the Marxists do not call themselves an "elite" and their apparatus a "state," that they call it "the Party," or the "Supreme Soviet," or the "Politburo." It functions as a state without filling the state's role: protection of the common good. Also, it makes no difference whether the Marxists claim to have abolished "politics," which in their definition is only one thing: the interplay of hostile classes. In leveling and controlling the population there is indeed no politics—as in the life of the *polis*—but politics has not ceased to exist in a deformed, corrupted, and monstrous way; it is concentrated in the Politburo, where the struggle takes place for supremacy, influence, power, life, and death. At levels lower than the Politburo, formal politics is indeed nonexistent, in the sense that citizens have no right to express their aspirations, interests, and opinions. Yet they too are affected by the power conflict at the summit, as thousands of them are killed or sent to prison camps in the wake of the temporary victory of this or that faction.

In this manner, not only the state and politics are corrupted and turned into caricatures of themselves: the entire life of society is deformed and deflected from its natural pursuits. Hegel insisted on a wide role for the individual within the framework of family and civil society, but such a role is erased in the Marxist regime, as are cultural enterprises, which also are controlled and determined by the absolute political monopoly of the leading group. Since the common good is conceived as the good of that group only, the other citizens are either reduced to the condition of serfdom to the regime or (a minority of them) strive to secure for themselves a place under the Marxist sun. This strife degenerates, by necessity, into a *bellum omnium contra omnes,* worse than in Hobbesian society, in which men fight other men until the frictions and fear compel them to enter a contract and entrust one man with the guardianship of "collective security." Under the Marxist regime, the precontractual general fear does not cease, but all continue to fear the state as well, a false guardian. And since the state is ubiquitous, suspicious, and cruel, each citizen continues to fear his fellowmen too, as the state's possible agents. Hence the permanent struggle to reach positions of power, a temporary niche in the never ending life and death scramble for privileges, including the privilege (*not* the right) to survive.

From books, personal reports, and other types of witnessing documents, one pictures the situation as the moral deformation of the citizens. Solzhenitsyn describes it as "a society of the permanent lie," but this implies many things besides: theft for survival, betrayal of acquaintances and friends, denunciation of innocents, victimization of all by everybody. Communism not only fails to encourage virtue, it educates for vice, sin, and crime. Ordinary social acts become "negative" against the background of everyone's awareness that the authorities are always listening: at the workplace, in schools, in social clubs, in the lines in front of shops, among friends.

Marx did not invent conflict among men, but together with Hegel he erected it into a general, explanatory system of human behavior. The nucleus of the system is contained in what in Hegel's work is the "dialectics of master and slave," a model that Marx applied to the struggle of classes. The master and the slave are at the origin of society as such; they signify the radical attempt of both to conquer the other, to subjugate him. The master has a built-in advantage, but since he disregards the slave as a subject, the latter slowly turns the situation to his own favor. The outcome is the slave's victory, which, however, works for the abolition of both mastership and slavehood in a reconciled humanity.

No doubt that Marx took the ideas of class struggle, the dictatorship of the proletariat, and the classless society from the Hegelian myth. Alexandre Kojève, who called himself a Marxo-Hegelian, is perhaps the most competent insider to give an account of the master–slave dogma, on which he commented at length in his study of Hegel's thought.[39] The philosopher (Kojève has Hegel in mind) was no longer satisfied with the traditional objectives of his discipline: evidence, intuition, or clear and distinct ideas; he had grasped the necessity to participate in history, that is, to engage in political action. The *being* that he studied is really a *becoming,* and this process, this flux, can be ascertained only in history. The processes of becoming, explicit in conflictual situations, and engendered by the contradictions inherent in all situations between what *is* and what *is not yet* but is emerging. The conflicts are overcome by elimination of the contradiction and, also, the contradictor. (This is no sin or crime; it is the way history proceeds, over which morality has no hold since morality is always that of the dominant but already declining class.) The action of solving the contradiction is twofold: against nature (work) and against man (struggle).

> The Truth emerges from this dialectics when the process is completed: history comes to its final conclusion in the universal and homogeneous State. This satisfies all citizens, thus it excludes all possibility of negating action, hence of all negation.... It is only by proceeding in this manner that philosophy will make its way towards absolute knowledge.[40]

This line of thought demonstrates, with all the clarity required, the inexorability of history as proposed by Hegel and Marx—its divinization. This, in turn, explains the insignificance of man's role in history, in the state, in political and cultural life, and it justifies the "philosopher-leader" in his arbitrariness in moving citizens on history's chessboard according to the "laws of historical necessity."

More subtle or less fanatical than Marx, Hegel foresaw that his philosophy was not to be the last one, that speculation and history, in typical Hegelian fusion, would continue indefinitely. In rather obscure or perhaps only veiled terms, he suggested that those who are, as it were, left out of the scope of the state, and thereby of the realm of reason as well, must be integrated before the state can acquire its full dimension as *thought*. Those who were left out—from participation, from consumership, from dignity—are the proletariat (though Hegel did not use the term). Their incorporation with the state will not happen without the dialectical conflict, which is the law of the "spirit" as it manifests itself in the concrete universe.

History has not ended with either Hegel or Marx, nor according to their prescription. Political thinking also continues, but since our intention is not to register its complete chronicle but to mark the high points at which Catholic thought is challenged, we do not accompany political thought in all its meanderings. References to it will be made throughout chapters 3 and 4.

However, this chapter should not close without a general inventory, up to Marx. A somewhat simplified overview may note that ancient (mostly Greek and Roman) political thought dealt with the *state* as the central fact of public life, and that medieval thought put the accent on *God* as the source of power. This generalization can be defended as referring to the two main contributions to political thought in the West: the classical and the Christian. What has been, then, the axis of modern political thought?

Without hesitation we answer, the *individual*. Not the people, the nation, or the monarch, but the individual, theoretically detachable from God and the community, and served by both through endowment by the Supreme Being with "inalienable rights" and through positive laws, passed by the community, so that he may pursue his interests.

Spinoza offers a good illustration of the modern view. "Democracy is the universal union of men," he wrote, "who, together, in collegiality, have a total right to everything over which they have power.... No one is obliged to serve one of his peers."[41] Spinoza went so far as to suggest that every new collectivity takes shape initially as a democracy; then, by progressive seizure and concentration of power, it is transformed into aristocracy and monarchy. Thus democracy, for Spinoza, is the natural state for men, just as monarchy was held to be natural for the ancient and the medieval thinkers.[42]

Yet it is notorious that a political science, built on the individual as its first principle, is fragile and untenable. Politics is about the relationship among men and therefore about what binds them: the common good, its moral dimension, and its guarantee in the divine order. Thus it is not surprising that politics in the Western world increasingly took a *utopian orientation,* and that this orientation was strengthened after Hegel and Marx. Let us see the reasons.

Placing the individual in the center of political thought means that the objectives of the analysis are lost sight of, namely, the other political realities, less ephemeral than the individual. The political debate becomes subjective; it is derailed toward mental constructs in which emotions, ideologies, and personal fancies play a substantial part. The greater the distance from political *realism* (as distinct from *nominalism* [see our discussion in Chapter

1]), the more are thinkers prompted to handle politics as something elastic, compressible, and extendable; unreal; dependent on subjective evaluations and preferences. The result is impatient abandonment of politics as dirty and untouchable and its substitution by theories that the formulator can shape at will. Hence arises the fashion of fabricating utopias, "perfect societies" placed in a timeless time, consisting of "citizens" no longer blessed and cursed by ordinary human features. Elaborating such constructs, the theoretician grants himself and his illusion-chasing fellows the luxury of dealing with puppets—or robots—which respond (better, of course, than human beings would) to his manipulative devices. In Utopia, everything is orderly, harmonious, and happy, with the added advantage, as seen in Rousseau, Hegel, and Marx, that it remains forever so, since the stage is set once and for all, and the characters of the ironclad plot possess only such traits as the stage director has implanted in them.

Now political science of the last hundred years has been dominated by this utopian orientation. There have been, naturally, great thinkers on political matters, but mostly such that accepted the classical and Christian tradition and were not in the least embarrassed to pursue the old inquiry into the ever mysterious nature of the "political thing" and political man. Others chose the way of fashion: politics as the science of behavior, as the science of "the revolution," as the science of class or other occult interests, as activism in view of this or that end, whether the triumph of an ideology or the building of a reconciled mankind in a world-state. These latter endeavors are only tangentially *political*. While they are not theories in the traditional sense, they partake, as fashionable systems, in the current political controversies, often dominating them. Thus we, as contemporaries, cannot ignore them; they are parts of the world in which we live. The Christian is surrounded with these ideology-inspired theories and systems, with the issues and isms they propose.

In the next chapter we shall discuss the Christian view of politics and the state, together with the temptations into which misconceived and misapplied Christian thought may lead.

Chapter 3
Three Temptations of
Catholic Political Thought

It is evident from the foregoing that Catholic reflection upon political matters is not only an integral part of Western political philosophy, it is the main avenue out of the impasse in which this science has found itself since the Renaissance. Let us recall what we said of Thomist political thought at the close of chapter 1: that God does not work through primary agents. In other words, he does not create individuals whose mere agglomeration constitutes the state (democracy), nor does he intervene directly in setting up and governing the state through his Church and churchmen (theocracy). The Thomist reconciliation of these extreme positions, embodied in medieval theories presents the state as a secondary agent: The people give their consent, they do not rule; they act, but these actions are not the cause of the transfer of authority from God to ruler, only the *condition* of the transfer. Authority does not rest, even for a moment, with the people; in other words, there is no contract first, then a contractual designation of the ruler. By the fact of sociability, men give up the best part of their *political* essence in favor of the laws which guarantee the good management of this part—and only this part. Thus there is no contract, since the individual could not have withheld his consent; and the state has not become either totalitarian or tutelary, since the citizen retains a substantial part of his rights to individual pursuits—even, tacitly, to his unvirtuous inclinations. Be it understood, however: *qua* citizen, not *qua* Christian.[1]

These are the general outlines of Catholic thought about the state. This thought is the fruit of the Thomist synthesis, grown out of centuries of controversy, and of course unable to resolve the controversies of subsequent centuries, to our day. The post-Thomist centuries recapitulated, to a large extent, the old debates, but also added new problems and developments to which the neo-Thomists of modern times sought answers, without, however, providing the kind of thoroughly elaborated monument that St. Thomas, building on the foundations of classical thought, had constructed. Our task in this chapter is then twofold:

a) To describe the errors into which Catholics may be led, first, by misunderstanding their politically applicable principles and, second, by combining this misconception with the errors of modern, non-Catholic, political thought; and

b) To describe the principles on which modern political thought rests and to confront them with the Catholic point of view.

Out of these descriptions, we trust, will arise the possibility of a new synthesis, not Thomist in power and scope, yet an outline and more: a guideline in the present situation.

Catholic political thought, or for that matter *any* political thought, can never be applied in its purity in this imperfect world. Politics has been called "the art of the possible," which means that human interactions, to which we may add divine action in its various manifestations, render all situations complex to the point where political theories seem like very narrow paths in a vastly diversified landscape. Yet one should not underestimate theory, whether correct or not. The metaphor of a narrow path in a vast landscape does not hold up long, because theory also modifies every part of the landscape. Those who pass through, even if they stay a while, accept the modified landscape; that is, they contemplate it through the "glasses" provided by the theory. They do not know that other perspectives are also available. Concretely, and for our discourse, this means that living under a regime that is based on a wrong theory is not necessarily perceived by the citizens as a bad regime and a bad theory; chances are that they would not perceive any causal connection between theory and regime. Thus it is by no means sufficient to point out an error; it is naive to expect that people, by and large, would recognize it as such, see its influence on the regime they otherwise reject, and want to change the theory, even though they may want to change the regime, and so on.

Error, political-theoretical error too, has its staying power because it is probably the logical conclusion not of the theory but of a partially grasped theory, or the grasp of only part of the theory. In Catholic thought, we may distinguish three such errors, logical consequences of a partial view of man as he is according to the Church's teaching.

1) The first error follows from the assumption that *redeemed man is in no need of politics*. This position was held by the Gnostics,[2] the "elect" who rejected politics (the state) as the sphere of matter, movement, and uncleanliness—in other words, involvement with bodily, mundane interests. Ever since the Gnostics, all sorts of heretical sects have advocated the same theses, believing that the true Christian becomes at baptism a pure spirit who has internalized the religious laws and is therefore exempt from the constraints placed on him from outside by an institution, by the Church. The heretic rebels against the Church, in which he sees a contradiction: between the spirit and those who insist on a corporeal garb for it. When he considers not the Church but the secular government (the state), in addition to religious heretic he becomes a political anarchist, rejecting laws and institutions with the same argument: his transformation into a "spiritual" being has made him perfect or almost perfect and laws are only for imperfect creatures, who are still immersed in

the world of flesh and physical temptations. This was and is the position of many medieval and modern sects. From the Cathars in Provence to Wyclif's followers, from the Brethren of the Free Spirit (in the Rhineland) to the Levellers and Winstanley's Diggers in England (seventeenth century), the cry went up that only Christ is judge, that no human, king or court, may pass judgment on Christians.

It is understandable why many Christians are attracted to this antipolitical view, primarily those who conceive of their religion either as preaching the divine kingdom on earth or as having transformed individuals into saints. In both cases, politics becomes an ugly reminder that the world's christification is not yet an accomplished fact; it is indeed a refutation of such a possibility. Whoever cooperates with politics and worldly institutions and interests, contradicts, or at least slows down humanity's becoming divine. Concretely, since even Christians who reject politics realize that God's kingdom has not yet arrived, *they* become politicized, although they refuse to call their involvement by that name. Over against "rigid" and "hierarchical" institutions, they help promote some form of anarchy, radical democracy, or communism, judging these regimes to be closer to the Christian ideal, that is, closer to the abolition of political power. They do not accept the evidence that these regimes become quite despotic, precisely because they claim to be nonpolitical; yet they must deal with human beings whose created nature functions according to political structures in public, community life. Confronted with the evidence of inhuman despotism in anarchistic or Communistic regimes, the Christian who favors them argues that these are drastic remedies needed for the transition between a still not redeemed world and the imminent arrival of Christ's kingdom. Such arguments have been frequently put forward even by prestigious Catholic thinkers in our time, who were willing to accept the Communist regimes and their conquests as "God's punishment for the sins of the Christian-capitalist world." The resulting, "purged" Western world is supposed to be a better receptacle for Christ's teaching and kingdom.

Yet, as Reinhold Niebuhr understood it, "history is a long tale of abortive effort towards the desired end of social cohesion and justice in which failure was usually due either to the effort to eliminate the factor of force entirely or to an undue reliance on it."[3]

In truth, the two efforts very often work hand in hand, at least in modern times, when regimes and governments have assumed utopian expectations. Those ideologies which propose an elaborate method of eliminating injustice, as it is embodied in "oppressive" institutions, find out early in the process that the restraints without which there is no society must be exercised, and far more harshly than before, by new institutions (whose names, however, are changed beyond recognition). The refusal to apply force becomes, rather than moderate and rational, an application of brutal force, without any rational and humane limit.

Thus the error of the Christian whose intellectual case we are examining:

    a) He is either mistaken in regarding himself and other Christians (usually a group of like-minded people) as redeemed, or

    b) Even redeemed men are in need of political structures.

Concerning the first point, Christians have no ground for assuming that Christ's incarnation has transformed them into saints (and it is indeed by "saint" or its equivalent, "pure" or "elect," that heretical sects designate their members). Concerning the second point, Thomas Aquinas argued that even if man had not fallen, communities that are formed by human beings must be "political." He added that, in such a community, political authority would be exercised without constraints, since obedience would be freely given.

The proposition that redeemed man needs no politics is thus shot through with errors and inconsistencies, of both a theoretical and a practical order, and ultimately of a religious order. Does one have to remind Christians that Christ and Paul accepted the state—more than that, the *pagan* state—and that the early Christians, even while persecuted, cooperated with it? Nearer to us, Solzhenitsyn gave a Christian example of considerable magnitude and significance, among other writings in his *Letter to the Kremlin's Leaders,* written before his forcible exile—that is, on Russian soil, and not recanted since then. In this letter the Russian writer does not ask for abolition of the Soviet state, not even for abrogation of most of its harsh laws; he merely suggests the government's humanization—a rational act, he adds, because it is better for the leaders to initiate it on their own than later be compelled to do so by the peoples' uprising.

> Let the State remain authoritarian. But it should no longer be based on the mutual hatred of the classes, it should be based on the love of men. Let the leaders show humanity towards the whole nation, and first, charity towards the prisoners. . . . Let them accept the various religions, a free art and literature. . . . Let women not have to work, let wages be decent.[4]

At no point in Solzhenitsyn's writings is the legitimacy of the state denied. On the contrary, such a denial is the central notion of Marxists, who, after reaching power, multiply a thousandfold the evil features of tsarist and Mongol despotism, and the forms of other ancestral despotisms in other countires, turned over to Marxist rule. Yet the question remains: Do contemporary Christians have better reason than their forebears to propose a non-political community, the spiritual community of Christ, to replace the kingdom of this world?

Their religion teaches them neither optimism nor pessimism, but hope in an everlasting kingdom—and in the meantime the parallel course of good and evil upon this earth. Yet modern

Christian thought has suggested new perspectives, largely under the influence of the scientific worldview and the *unfounded* optimism it has generated. Christian thinkers, like Karl Rahner, Teilhard de Chardin, Paul Tillich, M.-D. Chenu, Jacques Maritain, have adopted a kind of evolutionism which tries to be Christian, that is based on the Church's tradition and magisterium, but turns into outright evolutionism, to which Christian texts are adapted for the sake of an orthodox appearance. It is obvious from reading such authors that behind this "Christian evolutionism" is yet another motive: adjustment of Christian thinking and institutions to an *ideal politics,* which would be, in fact, the abolition of politics as outlined above.

The time has come, according to these authors, to reformulate the Christian view of politics and history so as to insert Christians, bypassed by the recent centuries, in the "human mainstream," which is essentially secular, and to accelerate the mainstream by the addition of Christian energies. Thus a new emphasis is put on the this-worldly construction of the "City of God"—a parallel emphasis, one gathers, to the "edification of socialism" that some Christian thinkers envy and wish to emulate. The historian H.-I. Marrou phrases it with modesty:

> We are inserted in the fabric of history, carried by its flow, both active and passive because we submit to it as well as create it. Yet we do not know history fully, since it is not yet written.[5]

The views of others are much bolder. Karl Rahner distinguishes "two Christianities": one is the religion of the "absolute future" and the other proposes an "inner-worldly future." The object of the first is God, that of the second a future planned by man. This thesis means either nothing new, that is, free human action under God's providence, or it is a clumsy adaptation of Marxist social planning. In this case, it suggests that Christianity has no objection to Marxist socialism, as long as the latter secures the free worship of God and does not confuse God with the state.

In his *Theology of Work*, Fr. M.-D. Chenu, the Dominican Thomist, goes much further. The whole structure of the modern world in the West today, he writes, has Christian inceptions; so Christians are perfectly prepared for, and should favor, the dawning of new dynamics, long innate in man and

> now suddenly brought to light in the revolutionary glow of a new civilization. . . . Socialism, even with its formidable implications, will lead to a wonderful communion in which man finds both self-realization and liberty.[6]

Perhaps the views of other, equally or more influential writers on the subject may be dispensed with. Let us note that literature of this type has grown to enormous proportions since at least the beginning of the century, but particularly during the past twenty-five years. In his book on the main trends of this literature, the Argentinian Julio Meinvielle was able, a quarter of a century ago, to limit his study to the "classics," as is indicated by his title, *De Lamennais à Maritain.*[7] But the promulgation of the encyclical *Humani Generis* by Pius XII (1950), in which the pope condemned the "progressivist" and evolutionist ideas of a number of theologians, then Vatican II, have opened a floodgate for these writers; the texts reached the proportion of an avalanche after the Council. The same trend prevails throughout. Meinvielle quotes Maritain who anticipated Rahner, thus linking two generations of theologians:

> In regard to the Kingdom of God and of eternal life, what makes the difference is the acceptance or rejection of religious dogma. In regard to the terrestrial

city the difference is between the acceptance or refusal of mankind's historical vocation.[8]

"Mankind's historical vocation" is an ambiguous phrase, but it
is present, variously treated and commented on, in the writings
of Marrou, Hans Küng, Helmut Gollwitzer, Teilhard,
Hulsbosch, Bultmann, etc. It transcribes, in more or less excessive terms, a general belief of our age, and a particular belief of
Christians in modern times, in the soon-to-arrive redemption
through political means, the kingdom in which fraternity will be
substituted for politics and the classless society for the state.
Earlier, we asked whether the Christian has more cogent reasons
today to expect that the spiritual community of Christ might
replace the kingdom of this world. The answer is, of course, no.
In time, we simply do not know what tomorrow will bring; in
eternity, we are always as near or as far from the fulfillment of
God's will as at any other point. Nor can it be said that the
present expectation is a sign of increasing and intensified Christianity; the age is definitely secular, desacralized; insane myths
cross our firmament like shiny, vanishing meteors. Why then the
belief by Christians that not only the time of redeemed man but
redeemed society is near?
    I think the answer is to be found in the extraordinary growth
in the last two centuries of *secular society,* with its myriad
ideologies which do not so much contradict one another as express the same thrust: away from theocentric man, toward autonomous man.[9] On the surface, secular society makes great
strides. It has managed to desacralize—that is, impose its ideology
on—all parts of the planet that until recently were theocentric societies: tribes, clans, nations. The flaws of the secular society, foreseen by great minds even in the eighteenth century (for
example, Vico and Goethe), did not appear until quite recently;
so we are still impressed with its achievements rather than
alarmed at its failures.

Christians, whose beliefs and convictions have been subjected to a severe strain, in proportion as the secular society and way of life progressed and expanded, had to choose between this alternative: go over to the secular society or find a compromise solution between their religion and their way of life. We are obviously not concerned here with the first category, which, by definition, has abandoned our discourse. The second category, not quite de-Christianized, but attempting to desacralize Christianity (for its own comfort!) on the lines prescribed by secular society, has formulated the *heresy of Modernism* and its sequels. In the present phase, this neo-Modernism appears as a much aggravated version of the earlier heresy, so branded by Pius X. In Maritain's words (alas, sounded too late): Compared to its present form, the earlier form of Modernism was mere hayfever; today it is plague and cholera combined.

"Redeemed society" is the new heaven for many Christian writers, who, in part unaware, elaborate their theses on the tracks laid down by the secular ideology and its escort, the scientific worldview. Society's redemption is expected from evolution (Teilhard), socialism (Chenu), a one-world, pluralistic system (Rahner), democracy (Maritain), an ecumenic religion (Küng), dialogue with Marxism (Gollwitzer), and so on.

Such theses have nothing to do with politics; they are *secular-eschatological* guesswork, garbed with political terminology. In their scope, the texts we refer to oscillate between the two medieval branches of the political alternative: democracy and theocracy. We saw the Thomist answer: rejection of both. There is no reason to modify this answer today.

2) The second political error to which Christians as such may be attracted is the exact opposite of the first. Not only are men not redeemed, *they are wretchedly sinful, thus deserving, for their punishment and ultimately for their good, to be ruled by a harsh government*. The thesis "redeemed man needs no politics" leads,

as we said, to *democracy* and its variants: anarchy and communism, finally to despotism over unruly men. The thesis "harsh government for sinful men" leads to *theocracy,* because their sins make men so disobedient to God that in this world only God's direct representatives are able to discipline them.

The term "theocracy" points in modern times to Calvin (in Geneva, in Scotland, in Massachusetts) and generally to a trend within Western Christendom which is as alive today as its opposite (discussed as the "first error"). At a superficial glance, only Calvin qualifies under the "second error," and even this may be questioned in the light of the founder's attack on his contemporaries who "would that men should live pell-mell like rats in straw," that is, those who, like Luther, believed that in a society of true Christians no law would be needed (*Institutions,* 1541). And it is true that Luther came close to committing the "first error." He believed, like St. Augustine, that the ruler is generally a fool or a rogue, and although we should obey him, we must admit that the less we have of man-made laws the better. "Love needs no law," Luther believed.

Yet when we look more closely, we find Luther and Calvin not far from each other's position on matters of state and politics. Both held that original sin "so corrupted human understanding [*not* just human will!] that man is alienated from divine justice, unable to think or imagine anything but evil and corrupt things. His heart is poisoned by sin and can only produce perversities. Even the occasional good is mere vanity and hypocrisy" (*Institutions,* chapter II). This rebellious lot must be coerced by government to make it conform, at least outwardly, to divine will. Calvin's follower, Beza, spelled out the aim of government even more clearly: The chief and ultimate end of human society is not that men should live together in peace but that, living in peace, they should serve God. Thus the magistrate must be centrally concerned with religious matters and "suppress by the power of the sword those who obstinately contemn it and form sects."[10]

This is a clearly stated necessity of theocratic government—
to which it is useful to set in contrast the Thomist view. Aquinas
conceived the function of secular government to be the establishment for all citizens of such a level of security and well-being
as would liberate men for the pursuit of their true end. Thomas
too conceives this secular order under the Church's guidance;
but the crucial difference between him and the reformers is that,
in Thomas's view, men have retained, after the fall, enough of
their intellectual and moral integrity to be able to control their
actions rationally, and also the actions of their fellow men. Thus
Thomas sees both magistrate and citizens as rational beings,
capable of self- and mutual control, whereas Calvin sees the
citizens as an unruly pack of rats, at constant war with the
magistrates.

Why are the latter also not evil, sinful men? Because, we are
told, they are "predestined" men, members of the "invisible
Church," who follow Scripture only and who are filled with, and
preach, the word of God. Luther, less articulate on matters of
civil society, was in basic agreement. For him, too, politics is
expandable; Christians must live in an invisible community, and
institutions, whether Church or state, should be shunned. But
since there *are* such political institutions, the Christian does best
to accept the domination of "fools and knaves," following God's
commands—which, by the way, he does not even understand,
with his unruly and obscured intelligence, but to which he nevertheless submits. In consequence, Luther and Calvin moved on
the same line, and the second merely explicated the premises
that the first left as the essence of political Protestantism, without
working out their inherent logic.[11]

In the context discussed here, the "harsh government" advocated (inherently or explicitly) by the early reformers is theocratic government, the rule of the "elect" who speak directly with
God's voice. After Calvin, in Presbyterian circles in England,
Scotland, and later in Massachusetts, Calvinists demanded the

"minimal state" (as it is called today), since all could claim the status of elect, with the Bible in hand and observing frugal mores. Thus it was logical to switch the emphasis from the theocratic state to a "theocratic society," under a government with reduced functions. The ideal of the "good society," a strong sociological force in the thinking of Americans, is derived from it. This for a while was also the trend in continental Europe, where the Huguenots turned the Calvinist tenets into a republican doctrine. The two trends soon fused in a kind of *secular Calvinism,* whose main stages are found in Rousseau's General Will and in the Jacobin ideology of the French Revolution. Having no moral restraints, human beings must be ruled in such a way as to make them virtuous against their self-will. The "magistrate," who enforces virtue from a theocratic but no longer Christian pedestal, is Robespierre. Thus, although "secular Calvinism" has acquired democratic credentials, the underlying principle remains that of theocracy. This is a way of saying that human beings do not possess qualities to organize themselves into a rationally functioning political society—but since the existence of such a society is indispensable and since all that really matters is salvation, the job of politics is best left to a severe elite.

Calvin's twentieth-century follower, the theologian Karl Barth, illustrates these assumptions and conclusions. It has been said of Barth that he is more orthodox than Calvin himself; while he is certainly representative of Genevan thinking, he also displays some of the contradictions inherent in "Calvinist politics." Like Luther, like Calvin, Barth argues that society is not really worth worrying about[12]; world history and political matters are fundamentally uninteresting and monotonous:

> Human society is either a company of highly individual members from which the crying wrongs that go with such a membership are never absent, or a kind of barracks, ruled by constraints, tediousness and stupidity, wherein right is wrong.[13]

What saves this statement from irresponsibility is that it contains the two extremes to which Christians are prone. The first half of the sentence declares that society is in a state of anarchy, the second half that it is ruled by despots. *Tertium non datur*. It is thus understandable that Barth does not want Christians to commit their souls and actions to such a silly enterprise. "I cannot admit," he writes, "that it is the duty of Christians or of the Church to give theological backing to what every citizen can, with much shaking of the head, read in his daily paper and what is so admirably expressed by Mr. Truman and by the Pope."[14] The voice is obviously Calvin's, who likened human beings to "rats in the straw," except that Barth, it seems at first, has no use for a harsh regime which would discipline these rats. But it only seems so. In a complete turnabout, Barth's contempt for politics and state becomes eager solicitude for the war against Hitler and for socialism!

Note that it is the same thinker—an immensely prestigious one—who dismissed political preoccupations *and* put his trust in men, who are unable to make sense of their temporal life yet are expected to be deeply worshipful of God. Such contradictions are surmounted with silence—and Barth then declares that the "Church must stand for social justice in the political sphere." And in choosing between the various socialistic possibilities, the Church will always choose the movement from which it can expect the greatest measure of social justice (leaving all other considerations on the side).[15] Barth's favorable regard of communism (he lists "radical Marxism" as one of the "socialistic possibilities" from which the Church must choose its version of "social justice") can be explained only by his Calvinistic bent for harsh government. Hence the leap, without intermediary steps, from indifference, to politics, to favoring the cruelest caricature of a theocratic regime.[16]

These contradictory positions may be explained with reference to Barth's theology. God is the "Absolute Other" (*totaliter*

aliter); he is not in history, not in the public affairs of men, not (presumably) in their concern with civilization. This clarifies Barth's conviction that politics is without interest. Indeed, if man has no superior reference for his public actions, if he must concentrate exclusively on his individual salvation, then history remains utterly uninteresting—as he says, "monotonous." *Or*—but not at all paradoxically—history, abandoned by the "totally other" God, becomes rat-infested straw, a free-for-all where the strongest rat prevails. The indifference of the many leads to the tyranny of one.

Ironically, Barth praised communism for never having attempted "to reinterpret or falsify Christianity, or to shroud itself in a Christian garment." Insofar as this is true—and it is not quite true—we understand the reason even if Barth did not: communism *is* anti-Christianity. It is the logical end when, at the beginning, men are judged to be too evil and too stupid to constitute themselves in society.

3) The third error is the most deceptive because the most ambiguous. The first and second errors so obviously follow from unorthodox positions that their detection is relatively easy. The one we are going to examine now does not refer to the "redeemed man" or the "corrupt man"; it refers to a thesis which is pagan in origin, and thus it is not the political transposition of a heretical view. The objection against the third error is that it is simply not a Christian but a pre-Christian position although the fact that it exercises a certain attraction on Christians proves its usability for the Christian political discourse, broadly understood.

Even the Scholastics called the state a *communitas perfectissima*. At a time when words still had precise significance, the adjective did not mean "perfect" but "accomplished," "fulfilling its function." The state is destined for human beings to live their lives in a framework that is suitable for, as well as permits, the fullest individual and communitarian achievement. The idea came from Aristotle and Cicero, who indeed knew nothing higher in this world than the well-ordered polity; the individual who sought a still higher destiny was regarded by the Greeks as "divine" (a term differently used then and now). When the Scholastics spoke of the community as *perfectissima*, they used the term in the Aristotelian sense, not forgetting that in the Christian view the state is God's creation, thus not perfect *per se*—only fulfilling, in the corporate order, the role for which it was created. Man's scope is greater and higher than what the state offers; yet, as Josef Fuchs notes, "family and State, politics and economics are developments of life that are prefigured in man's being."[17]

This is an important observation in view of the content of the "third error," for a number of thinkers have contended that *the state is the highest expression of human endeavor*, which is, as we saw, the thesis of the best of pagan philosophers, and therefore a pagan thesis. In recent times, Hegel and Joseph de Maistre were expositors of this point of view, as we have pointed out. Let us again try to understand where they contradict the Catholic position and where we must draw the line between their *statolatry* and the Catholic recognition of the state as an essential component of the good life.

Hegel held that morality, like religion, is a subjective feeling, capable of great achievements (unselfishness, sacrifice), but without impact on the course of history and the collective development of mankind. "Objective morality" is the one which is effective in the state, the embodiment of the "ethical idea." For the individual, then, "true morality" is membership in the state, what Aristotle would call "citizenship in the *polis*." Only the state reveals the "ethical idea"; only in communion with the state is one able to know morality.

The difference with the Catholic concept is, again, obvious. The human being possesses the ability to acquire natural knowledge of morality; he does not need the state to reveal it to him. This is genuine intellectual knowledge, resulting from true insight into an intelligible object, the *good*. If God were an arbitrary being, as Ockham and his followers held, and would affix the label "good" now on this, now on that object, the state might indeed be the only source of practical certitude: in the chaos created by a capricious God, man would have recourse to the state, the highest corporate reality, for guidance. This is exactly what happens in the modern totalitarian state; the state (or whoever speaks in its name, for example, the Party) has *officially* become the exclusive source of morality, the only oracle of good and evil.

However, the definition of what is good is not given us by God's "arbitrary" will, it is taken from his being and revelation. Augustine said that goodness (as well as other ideas) is eternally in the mind of God, and thus not changeable or changed by a divine arbitrariness. And since there is between God and man the connaturality of creator to created being, man can know what is good by analyzing his own being and nature. Even while committing evil acts, man knows (unless he is mentally deficient or otherwise impaired) that he commits evil. He may regret it or rejoice in it (for example, in acts of vengeance), but at all times he is able to measure the moral quotient of what he does.

Hegel is of a different mind about these things. His state is powerful because it usurps and absorbs cognitions and functions that do not belong to it. Not only morality becomes "objective" (that is, efficient) within it, but also religion and freedom. Separate from the state, religion *prevents* the divine spirit from penetrating the human sphere through the state, the instrument par excellence of this penetration. Religion remains a set of subjective emotions and images whereas the state transforms them into throught and reason. Similarly, the state alone is objectively free; the individual's freedom is arbitrary, partial. The state is the supreme historical achievement of the "world spirit"; it is the *objective universal*. Only the state thinks; only the state can be the object of total reflection.

Thus, according to Hegel, the Catholic religion alone holds up fulfillment of the state by claiming, exclusively for itself, the domain of the sacred, leaving the profane sphere to the state. This halving, this truncating of the state, withholds its true potential: self-comprehension as universal reason. In contrast, Protestantism offers a satisfying conciliation, indeed more: a fusion of religion, philosophy, and state, the latter being the dialectically highest synthesis of the former two.

Thus if Christianity did not exist, the Hegelian state would be the modern equivalent of the Aristotelian *polis*. In the *polis*, no religious concerns were separate from the official cult; the various mystery cults were conceived as private associations with esoteric interests, like Freemasonry and Pentecostalism today. Freedom and morality were also expressions of citizenship; they were civic virtues that favored the state and promoted its cause. When Alcibiades pushed his licentiousness so far as to mutilate the Hermes statues in a drunken revelry, on the eve of the fleet's departure for Sicily (414 B.C.), this was not interpreted as an individual act of license but as a grave insult to the gods and a bad omen for the Athenian naval undertaking.

We find a similar attitude of reverence for the "divinities" of the state in the political philosophy of Leo Strauss and some of his followers. There is an uncomfortable undertone in Strauss's contention that the true political philosopher reverences what the state reverences, does not desecrate what the state holds sacred, and so on. This is inacceptable and, in light of Strauss's adherence to the Socratic stance, it sounds contradictory. It is inacceptable because the individual is not bound to reverence the laws of the state he considers immoral, for example, abortion laws. And it is contradictory because Socrates did not reverence the divinities of Athens; he taught rather, what the city *ought* to revere. Strauss's statement makes sense only in the context of his opposition to the line of political thinkers from Machiavelli to Hobbes, Locke, Rousseau and Hegel, down to the "absurd dogmatism of certain (present-day) academic liberals or social scientists."[18] No matter how correct Strauss was in the battles he waged, or in his recommendation that the political philosopher not subvert the values of the state, the state he outlines resembles the Aristotelian *polis* more than the modern state, which, in spite of the modernist trends which devastate it, has incorporated in itself the fact of Christianity.

The Christian concept does not admit the notion that the state is an embodiment of the ethical life. We have seen (on preceding pages) ample evidence that the state is a creature in its own right and that without it, outside it, no lasting community may exist. On occasion we shall argue further that talk about the "minimal state" or the state reduced to the role of a mere "guardian of law and order" is irresponsible and un-Christian. Nevertheless, a very sizable segment of the citizen's life is and should be conducted, if not outside and against the state, at least independently of it and irrelevant to its scope and objectives. St. Thomas warned against the kind of state that Calvin was to set up in Geneva: the state legislating and enforcing virtue. Even in areas where the aims of the state are compatible with the citizen's private aspirations, the latter is not expected to pursue them in spiritual communion with the state. In short, the Greeks' ideal state, containing all individual endeavors and without reverence for the transcendent, would be, if transferred to modern times, a totalitarian state, an object of adoration. This is so because the intervening lesson of Christianity has lifted the citizen beyond the state's scope, in denial of the state's totalist aspirations.

Let us add an epilogue to our discussion of the three errors which tempt Christians when they speculate about the state and politics. None should be considered as taking its origin in pure theory; each is at various times prompted to surface among men by concrete circumstances. The rejection of Church, state, institutions, and laws by the "redeemed," or "pure," or "elect" is based on a wrong interpretation of Scripture, doctrine, and magisterium, to be sure, but it also translates a dissatisfaction with Church policy and the laws of civil society. As we have seen, the Church in the twelfth century became attentive to these alarm signals and responded to them not merely with the persecution of heretics but also by taking the populace more into the life of the Church and by authorizing the mendicant orders.

The error which follows from the assumption of man's "totally corrupt nature" was, among other things, the result of the misinterpretation of Augustine's teaching about rulers as a gang of bandits. Augustine admitted the possibility of a just state, but his epigones darkened his somber views concerning man's weakness for sins of the flesh, views inherited from his Manichaeist days. An immediately acting factor on Luther and Calvin was the way in which the papal court, penetrated by the Renaissance spirit, handled the concept of sin: as a light matter, easy to remedy. In truth, the Jesuits of the seventeenth century turned this indulgent approach into casuistry, the method (caricatured by Pascal and Molière) which practically explained away sin by arguments taken from what we call today "situation ethics": a sin could be pardoned by or because of, the status of the sinner in society or in particular circumstances.

The third error, that of imposing a variation of the pagan state on Christians—and, generally, on the modern world—is partially explicable by the eighteenth- and nineteenth-century insistence on reducing the functions and role of the state to a minimum, in the name of a wide, democratic distribution of power and the "inviolability" of individual rights. "The ideal of an individualist and liberalist society," writes Rommen, "becomes the depreciation and minimizing of the State, and the exaltation of laissez-faire philosophy."[19] Not only did abuses continue to be committed in the name of "laissez-faire" (against all who were prevented from acting freely), but the state itself was harnessed to the interests of the new bourgeoisie, the proponent and the beneficiary of the liberal doctrine.

The reaction—often degenerating into overreaction—came in the early nineteenth century. In his *Elements of Statecraft,* Adam Müller wrote: "The State is not an artificial organization, it is not an invention by men, destined to be useful to the citizen and serve his pleasures. . . . The State is indispensable, based on human nature."[20] Earlier, the Protestant theologian, Schleiermacher, called the state a "work of art," a simile that Carl Schmitt was to use in his *Der Begriff des Politischen* (The Concept of Politics, 1928), where he analyzed the dangerous shortcomings of the liberal concept of the state. Hegel already had written in reaction to Rousseau's contract theory, and others were to work out further implications. Let us note among them Ferdinand Tönnies, who in order to save the state from absorption by civil society formulated the distinction between *Gesellschaft* and *Gemeinschaft,* the first being civil society, the second the tradition-bound, quasi-irrational, organically grown, and humanly felt and lived community. Evidently, Tönnies found in the state more affinity with the *Gemeinschaft* than with the *Gesellschaft.* In the latter, Tönnies wrote, the typical relationship between citizens is the act of the "merchant who buys money with money, through the medium of commodities."[21]

Müller, Tönnies, Schmitt, and Spengler were not, like Hegel, ideologues of the neo-pagan state; they reacted to an ideology which proposed the liquidation of the state. In this endeavor they were joined by writers from other nations: Benedetto Croce in Italy, Fustel de Coulanges and Charles Maurras in France, etc., who contributed their ideas, often colored by the political situation in their countries. Thus, quite often, what started as a defense of the idea of the state against its liquidators ended with a nationalist thesis, a typical product of our ideology-ridden epoch.

Chapter 4
The Catholic Position

After examining the three political temptations to which Christians are likely to succumb—we added the "epilogue" to suggest that this may have not only ideological causes but causes that are created by circumstances—let us outline the Catholic position.

There are two parts to this position, one which explains and justifies the existence of the state, the second which examines its internal structure. We saw in the preceding chapter the Thomist reconciliation of two positions, the "democratic" and the "theocratic," which were the most popular before his time and remained so afterward, though in various disguises. This permanence shows that the Thomist thesis is not merely the child of circumstances; it goes to the heart of the question and presents the only acceptable solution for the Catholic mind. But as our epilogue showed, concrete circumstances have their own weight; their impact enters naturally in the formulation of theories.

In the political realm, God does not act either directly through individuals (primary agents) or his own intervention, but through a secondary agent, the state. Human beings are so created that their nature functions to its full extent only in the company of their fellows, and not merely in random encounters and associations but in durable and structured communities. In fact, temporary, *ad hoc,* and limited associations are made possible through the existence of the secular corporation of the highest order, the state. In other words, civil society, the society formed by and for the transactions of economic and associative character, always finds itself within the framework of the state. This is also why anarchist and libertarian practice must always fail.

The multitude cannot govern, yet the state was created for their good. They *will* this good, and cannot *not* so will; however, it is for them to determine what kind of state shall govern them, and only such a state which has their approval is legitimate. The process of legitimation is not necessarily expressed through the vote; it may be expressed by other means also. Yet the authority actually to govern does not rest with the citizens; they are only the channels through which God grants it to the ruler. Let us quote here the conclusion of chapter 1:

> By the fact of sociability, men give up the best part of their political essence in *favor* of laws which guarantee the good management of this part—and *only* this part. Thus there is no (social) contract, since the individual could not have withheld his consent; and the state has not become either totalitarian or tutelary, since the citizen retains a substantial part of his right to individual pursuits.

Within the state the best regime is monarchy, writes St. Thomas. Authority is held by the secular ruler, but since the state has no jurisdiction over the citizens' virtue, nor even over their worship, the presence of the spiritual authority is essential, both for individual life and for the order and well-being of the state. Otherwise, let us add, another "religion" is bound to fill the vacuum which inevitably forms by the fact that no community can exist without an active moral authority. If this moral authority is not Christianity (we have in mind here the historically Western states, which, however, are not all located geographically in the West), it is provided by a "civic religion": in our century, a nationalist creed, Marxism, radical liberalism, etc.

The state is a rational construct for rational men, an organized network for the maintenance of order and justice, but its scope is only the *coordinated conduct* of its members, not the promotion of virtue. In the optimum case, the state creates conditions for the pursuit of virtuous life by legislating against the public display of sin, but it is not a pedagogue in the positive sense, as the neo-pagan view has it. The state cannot punish the sinner, but, informed by the moral authority, it can prevent the sinner from propagandizing his beliefs.

This issue immediately brings up a large number of related issues. If (for example) the state outlaws the display of pornography, should it pursue pornographic behavior in the private sphere also? Are pornographic magazines to be forbidden in public kiosks, but not bordellos in privately owned buildings? Should the state censor books, films, plays, newspapers, and public lectures or recitals? On what grounds: immorality or subversion, or both? Should the state pass legislation concerning the sex life of its citizens, that is, on abortion and contraception? What authority, within the state, should be appointed to define pornography, the public interest, subversion?

Let us say, anticipating discussion of some of these points, that there are no clear answers to every one of these questions—about which not merely the law (or its absence) is the key issue but also, in every case, prudential judgment. But prudence does not mean that if, in such cases, there is an upper limit, beyond which the state ought not go, there is no lower limit, below which the state would fail in its vocation if it did not act promptly and resolutely.

There are people in both camps. Some say that the state must protect itself as well as its citizens against licentiousness in public life, and even in the corridors that lead to the private sphere, and that, for efficacy, the best state is ruled by certified moral men, knit in the network of a moral government. Others say that it is sufficient to give the citizens a Christian education and Christian public examples; the state itself ought to remain neutral and leave to private associations, among them the churches, the task of influencing public affairs—indirectly.

In our estimation, both sides overstate their case and ignore the nature and functions of the state, which is not a mere mechanism of social protection or a morally and socially neutral agency. Creating it, God has given it a personality and powers of its own, and these powers are *extraordinary* from the citizens' viewpoint. It is the basic experience of all people, and the study of history testifies to it: The state has powers of compulsion which raise it above the social community. Its existence and presence cannot be equated simply with the sum of the citizens' interests and well-being. The state transcends these interests and the perspective of well-being, as if (but is this not indeed the case?) it had interests of its own which do not coincide, as the slogan has it, with the "camouflaged interests of a governing class" or of a more or less deserving upper echelon, near the fleshpots. One might speak of the "mystery" of power that comes into existence as soon as a state is constituted. Its organs acquire a weight, half of which may be derived from the sheer power of compulsion, but the other half comes from legitimacy and the awe it inspires. As Passerin d'Entrèves sums it up (*op. cit.* p. 12), in order to analyze the notion of the State, one must explain how force, first legalized as power, becomes legitimate authority.

The state presents itself, then, not as a visible God (as Hobbes's *deus mortalis* or de Maistre's direct manifestation of Providence), nor as a result of contract, revocable at will by any or all hypothetical contractants; it presents itself in three manifestations which underlie its functions but are not identical with these functions:

    a) Legitimacy,
    b) Symbols of legitimacy, and
    c) Coercive power derived from legitimacy.

For Christians, these manifestations are clarified by reference to man's nature and his fall. "The State," Joseph Fuchs writes,

is an absolute institution of the natural law. It would
have existed in paradise together with the authority to
govern. Man's freedom and equality would not have
excluded an organic structure of superiors and subjects.... As soon as men began to fall into sinful
egoism, the State, family, and institutions could no
longer depend on unselfish love, they required of
necessity certain means of coercion.[22]

The state is a divine creation, independent of original sin, yet
its coercive powers and the awe in which it is held increased after
the fall. Its legitimacy has also changed, insofar as it must deserve its domination, which is no longer derived from its mere
existence. In the eyes of the citizens, the state is legitimate when
they perceive that it tends to the common good and governs
according to reasonable laws. While occupancy and power are
sufficient for the affirmation of sovereignty, legitimacy has a
double root, superadded to the exercise of sovereignty: rule
according to traditional patterns, consecrated by time and usage
and wide acceptance by the ruled, who comprehend the nature
of the link between them and the ruler. As Cicero wrote, the
links which transform an aggregate of people into a State consist of respect for justice (*juris consensus*) and of the existence
of a common interest (*utilitaria communio*). This link receives symbolic expressions, also consecrated by time, by outstanding
events and common destiny, until such time that they become a
language in their own right, understood by ruler and ruled in
the same way they understand and speak the national tongue.
Only when legitimacy and the symbols of the community
meet can the state resort to coercive force, grasped in the name
of the common good—common, that is, to more than just the
contemporaries: to the deep interests of the community, its specific essence, historical vocation, its persistence in being.

As with bodily health, of which one becomes most aware when
illness strikes, so with legitimacy, symbols, and coercive power:
illegitimacy, alien symbols, and evil compulsion call attention to

them. Napoleon, the intelligent ruler, spent his entire time as emperor of the French (*not* of France, a title reserved for the kings, which again shows the power of symbols and symbolic language) seeking to establish his legitimacy. Legislating for the common good (the Code Napoleon, etc), the introduction of new sets of symbols (copied from the Romans, to whom the French were sensitive), and creation of a dynasty through marriage to the daughter of Europe's "most Catholic" emperor were steps he took to erase the revolutionary past and the memory of his own ascendancy, thanks to that past. Napoleon knew that the French Revolution, the epitome of illegitimacy, impinged upon his permanence in power—as Stalin knew too, and during the Second World War he rehabilitated Mother Russia and her past defenders and symbols, including the religious ones. Another illustration of the acquisition of legitimacy are the few sentences in Hungarian that Francis Joseph pronounced in 1867, when the Hungarian nation *accepted* him as king of the realm and bestowed St. Stephen's crown on him. It is on such occasions—and history is studded by them—that legitimacy is conferred and acquired, that its symbols are revived, and that the coercive power that derives from it is accepted without resistance. A proof of this is that conquerors implicitly act according to these "rules." "It is of utmost significance," Heinrich Rommen notes, "that the conqueror, to express the destruction of a real though invisible form of being represented in symbols, marks his conquest by the destruction of the symbols of the conquered political existence."[23] Not only foreign conquerors and occupants. Revolutionaries act in the same manner when they demolish and erase the old regime's symbols and replace them with their own—for example, the protestors and deserters who burned the American flag in the incidents of the 1960s and 1970s.

In every age, we intimated above, political and state matters must be reexamined, since no individual thinker, of even the greatest stature, can be expected to achieve more than supplying the general principles on which state and politics rest. Certain contemporary Thomists, who hardly learned their master's lessons, practically throw history overboard, saying it is not a science that can be taught. That history is not a science is true, but it is equally true that it provides the only fabric on which God and man indefinitely embroider new figures, none quite resembling the others and thus requiring new appraisals. Our situation (in the last quarter century in the West, in the United States) requires of us considerations and judgments which, even if there *are* preexisting models, cannot be automatically followed.

Let us begin with the most obvious illustration. When St. Thomas reflected upon the "best regime" (following the ancients) and concluded that it is monarchy, or when he reflected upon government as *not* created to enforce virtue, he found it natural that emperors and kings are the heads of state (though the Republic of Venice by then had a venerable past and was at the apogee of its power) and that the teaching of virtue may be entrusted to the Church, a central and secure institution in society. Neither of these two presuppositions is evident to us today. We have seen the passing of monarchy, the rise of republics, dictatorships, military regimes, totalitarian regimes, "guided democracies," "people's republics," and dozens of varieties of each. Some even conclude from this endless parade that the form of the regime is relatively unimportant; what matters is the economic policy they conduct. Or again, the Church, unceasingly since the beginning of the eighteenth century, has had a diminishing influence on citizens' choice of virtue or nonvirtue and, generally, on civilization. Today, the legislatures of all previously Christian nations enact laws which erect sin into the norm, and they do so in a social climate which is either largely indifferent to the intrinsic moral issues or, indeed, accepts and promotes immoral solutions.

In the terms of our previous discussion, the public faith is no longer Christian; it is shaped by the *civic religion* that Machiavelli proposed, after the fashion of pagan Rome: a religion which teaches that he who best serves the state best serves the gods.[24] But the prevailing civic religion cannot even be said to favor the state over the Church. The target of the modern revolt is no longer only the Church, it is the state as well—that is, anything that is solidly constructed, that has roots in the religious or the classical tradition. The "benefits" of the revolt are finally reaped by the secular world as such—by neither state nor Church— perhaps by a new entity: a monstrous one, bureaucratic and inert, ever present and shapeless, vacillating yet aggressive. Whatever its structures, the new entity must be classified as a temporal power whose impact is derived less from its specific weight than from its ideology. In a sense, then, the modern conflict does not oppose the state to the Church, but rather the Christian religion to a desacralized worldview which informs society and the state.

This is a fluid situation, but only because the nature of the ideological revolt is new, is not yet clearly grasped. Both Church and state are at present trying to conform to the situation and come to terms with it. But essentially the two protagonists remain state and Church, no matter how these two institutions will find themselves restructured in the future. However, the problem before the Christian citizen is new: Can he survive morally in a state that recognizes no spiritual transcendence that "competes" with itself (except in falsely pious lip service to "traditional values," best kept undefined), that is desacralized even in its function as protector of the common good and usurps, in a caricatural way, many functions of the Church, for example, in the moral order?

The separation of state and Church used to have at least the advantage of providing refuge to the Christian citizen when he engaged in activities that pertain to family, the education of children, and diverse aspects of cultural life. Although (in

America) such activities, under the Church's protective umbrella, were derisively described as belonging to a "ghetto," clear benefits were derived by the citizen from the fact that the line was clearly marked: the indifferent, morally neutral state versus the Christian Church. Today the state is not indifferent; it has a quasi-official ideology in secular humanism, which it takes for granted, and enforces in the public and increasingly in the private sphere as well. Two illustrations may help us gauge the nature of this ideology and its pervasiveness.

An elementary school district has been engaged in New Jersey in a project, financed by the federal government and supervised by federally appointed "researchers," to change "traditional sex roles" so as to prepare girls for leadership roles in society. For this purpose, one thousand school children, about ten years of age are divided into a test group and a control group, and the first group, is conditioned (through textbooks, movies, and various projects) so that girls perform "male jobs": lawn mowing, working in a paint shop, etc., and boys perform "female jobs": mending shirts, helping in the kitchen. The researchers have found that, even though these children have been growing up in an era that is conscious of "feminism" and "female rights," they act in the old manner; for example, girls seek out girls and boys seek out boys to play with. The idea is to break these "patterns" and have boys and girls play with children of the same age group or children who wear clothes of a similar color. The children, and presumably some parents, are unaware that "the teachers are supposed to take a more managerial role in the classroom" and that the researchers want to find out whether they can succeed in "reversing years of conditioning and changing the children's attitude with regard to the opposite sex."[25]

In Minneapolis, Fr. John Buchanan, pastor of Holy Childhood parish, was charged by the St. Paul Department of Human Rights with discrimination against a homosexual whose "gay rights" he allegedly violated when he refused to hire that person for a teaching position in the parish school. Fr. Buchanan's lawyer argued that this was a "religious case, a matter of City Hall telling a private Catholic school what to do," and not an issue of violation of human right.[26] The argument is significant since, in the prevailing ideological climate, the lawyer realized that his best chance was to invoke the separation of state and Church, and that he would lose if he invoked the moral position that children should not be exposed to homosexual influence.

Thus the semiofficial ideology (radically egalitarian, morally indifferent, which counts people merely as units, without their various qualities and defects) is so pervasive that it becomes almost impossible to protect children from immoral experiments upon their integrity as males and females, both the New Jersey and the St. Paul Minneapolis cases being just such experiments.

The principle of subsidiarity has broken down in the face of such ideology-inspired interference. Parents, whose task and prerogative it is to have a decisive say in their children's education, are pressured to yield this prerogative to *apparatchiks* of the state and its civil religion, who are commissioned by the state to reshape one of the most intimate sectors of a human being's world, his or her sex attitudes, and to change their heterosexual instincts into homosexual instincts, at an age when they cannot even resist. And this does not occur under a totalitarian government, which turns normal people insane in so-called psychiatric clinics or which experiments in biological selection. It occurs in the *model* democratic regime which intensely encourages "citizen participation."

The Thomist balance between the democratic and the theocratic state can be truly appreciated here, as we witness the former turn into the latter by a kind of natural logic. The reason why we hesitate to grasp the direction and speed of this transformation is that the terms used by the prevailing ideology have remained, by and large, identical with the accustomed terms: "freedom," "rights," "improvement," "participation," "processes of law," and so on. Yet "virtue" is now defined not by religious morality, it is defined by the semiofficial ideology. It consists of acceptance of the value system of the state, which itself is in the service of secular civilization. It is "virtuous" for all citizens to be like all other citizens, and among the "equalities" is sexual uniformity. No longer the "right to access to sexual satisfaction" (only a decade ago, this was the justification for the right to contraception, abortion, pornography by text and picture), now the state speaks in terms of leveling the sexes: All should be boys *and* girls, all should be homo-heterosexual.

The modern Western state is not just pagan, since the pagan state was organized around a cult; if it was unaware of a transcendent God, it adored deities, cosmic forces, and (like the Greeks) Fate, who stood above the gods, like a universal rule, inaccessible to manipulation. The modern state recognizes nothing above itself, and spurns the temptation to designate itself sacred, as the caesars and the rulers of the Near East empires once did. It replaces Fate with science and technology, manipulative devices through which the state can direct the citizens' lives and their future. More, the state—or the ideology it regards as the last word in human affairs, its ultimate reference—has made great strides in this century toward absorbing the Church as well, not with the purpose of sacralizing itself—in other words, not in order to create a caesaro-papist entity like that of the Byzantine emperors and the tsars of Russia—but prompted by the conviction that religion too is an instrument of government, an ideology in the service of the state. This conviction is hardly different from the Marxist theory, for example, that of the Italian theorist Antonio Gramsci, according to which the Leninist view must be refined and the citizenry permeated by Marxist ideology before its conquest of power.

Public life under our states presents, consequently, a desolate and flat landscape, where the inhabitants listlessly perform the functions that keep them alive, in spiritual desiccation. However, the question is not only a private one—the citizen's spiritual well-being—it is also a public one: Can the state survive without a transcendent dimension? Such a question never before arose in the history of man. All communities, from the most primitive— the Aborigines of Australia—to the most sophisticated—the Arab khalifates, the Western nations, the Chinese Empire—were so founded and organized as to recognize, at their axis in time, space, and spirit, a higher reference which sustained, justified, and admonished them.

We have mentioned legitimacy, sovereignty, their symbols, and the coercive power derived from them; and much of history consists of the combination, disintegration or destruction, and recombination of these elements of nationhood and statehood. The myriad styles in which these elements have been garbed have constituted factors of civilization and culture, insofar as they colored the national existence and gave a specific flavor to literature, art, music, law, statecraft, and religious experience, as well as other public manifestations. We should, I think, give credence to the view that the variety of nations, languages, and styles of life and art was willed by God, so that mankind might learn to praise him through a richly diversified experience. Patriotism itself, which is the projection of human loyalty on a large screen, acquires meaning, depth, and richness through the many objects—of the senses, emotions, the spirit—that belong to a nation and to which loyalty can be visibly attached. The same is true of religious worship. The catholicity of the Church does not exclude, it encourages local varieties of language, tradition, cults of saints, etc., by which believers become aware—at the same time—of their specificity and their membership in a universal corporation.

Only the modern state has consented to an absolute secularization, dragging behind itself all other institutions whose task is, in one way or another, to secure man's links to the sacred. Desacralization is followed by desymbolization and (why not?) loss of legitimacy, which is already perceptible as one sees millions of citizens who are increasingly disaffected, marginalized, and scornful of the state. In true secular fashion (that is, by confusing the essential and the secondary), the state blames unemployment, low wages, insufficient opportunities for sports and play. Consequently, billions of dollars are spent in programs set up by "researchers" and "experts" in an attempt to pacify the rebellious element. Hardly anybody dare think or say that the real cause of disaffection is the state's self-desacralization, its incapacity to offer a horizon other than more money and more playgrounds.

The conquest of the state by the civil religion is, assuredly, a temporary phenomenon, because no state can afford to be emptied of all meaning except concern with the material satisfaction of the citizens. Granted that, through its many agencies and channels the state can succeed in this partial endeavor, but recent events—in Poland and Iran, the latest illustrations—show that the citizens' other needs are just as important, and when they are neglected, the economic endeavor also fails. After all, rebellion against the state is not confined to the "economically disadvantaged" but includes the best categories, even the very rich and the privileged. The trouble is that the state's desacralization is pursued in the name of a desacralized civilization, which drags the churches down to its own level. Thus the citizen is not only aggressed upon by the state, he is confused by the churches, where he finds similar operative premises. The main collective task of the next few decades may be to disengage the Church from the state's embrace so as to restore her vocation.

This raises the complex question whether the Church must remain an essential ingredient inside and above the state, and whether such a role can be fulfilled if the Church lacks a certain power to permeate the civilization in which both society and state are enveloped. What are the various aspects of this issue in a nation where the separation of state and Church is stipulated by the Constitution?

The contemporary advocates of Machiavellian, Rousseauist, Hegelian (etc.) civil religion put forward more sophisticated arguments than the originators of the proposition. They must do so in a pluralistic-democratic society, where tolerance of all creeds is on the statute books and in the public mentality, and where the churches are regarded as equal with other public institutions, if not in regard to financial support from public funds at least in regard to participation in social uplift. These advocates argue that society in modern times has become morally better than societies were in the past, having absorbed, even if in nondogmatic form, the teaching of religion and having added to it two new elements: the enlightened liberal view of man and the scientific enterprise, including the social sciences, which has enormously enlarged the state's sphere of action. The conclusion is that religions have entered the social stream, have substantially improved the state's self-image and self-recognized pursuits, so that today the state has actually become state-and-Church in one, able to perform the functions that in the past had devolved separately on the two institutions. In its more brutal form, this proposition implies (as in Sweden) that the fiscal authorities penalize private charity so as to compel the citizens merely to pay their taxes, which then cover all welfare payments to the needy.

If we remember what Machiavelli said about the Christian religion—that it is a divisive and enfeebling factor—and compare it with what his present followers suggest, the difference does not seem important; only the verbiage has changed. The only real difference is that the churchmen of Machiavelli's time were scandalized by his theories, while many of today's Church intellectuals subscribe to the contemporary version. In their various idioms, Jacques Maritain, Karl Rahner, John Robinson, Hans Küng, ex-Fr. Montuclard have expressed at least partial agreement: the Church ought to withdraw, letting the state set and implement the socio-economic objectives, whether in economic planning, the education of children, or the moral issue of abortion. Or if the Church does not withdraw from public matters but wants to participate in them, it should do so according to a "theology of liberation," which regards Jesus Christ as a model revolutionary.

The Catholic position, however, cannot be other than insistence on the Church's specific mission in society, a mission that is penetrated by the divine mission of peace, love, and charity toward all men. For implementation of this mission the Church needs, in a certain sense, political power. It is not quite the same power that we have discussed with regard to the state, and certainly not the kind the Church possessed in the Middle Ages, pertaining to territory, armies, alliances, wars. Nor the power it has possessed in modern times, when practically every institution regards itself as part of a religious legacy, directed to the Church's service. In contemporary pluralist societies, the power of the Church can only be moral and spiritual, but it must so emphasize the moral and spiritual domain that it should be evident that society's integrity and survival depend on it. The result would be a modicum of mundane power as well, since by demonstrating that it is indispensable, the Church would acquire the means to communicate this fact to the state and to the agencies of society. One might say that this would be the reverse of some earlier situations, when political power was established first and spiritual power followed (for example, after the conquest of Mexico, Peru, and the Caribbean islands). Today our societies suffer from the (temporary) confusion that is still visible in the Church, which has rapidly lost the bases of its earlier power and has not yet reflected sufficiently on the possible bases that are now available.

Yet every day brings new proofs that state and society desperately need the Church's presence and active penetration in our crazy-quilt civilization. We have pointed out that the state has become unmoored and drifting. It has, of course, acquired powers it had never yet possessed, but it exercises them in an increasingly delirious manner, since there is no other institutional authority with which it could (or would be obliged to) share them. In comparison, the medieval conflict between papacy and empire, the spiritual and the secular, was not all that bad; it was an early system of checks and balances, and because of it the Lombard towns (for example) achieved independence and wealth as they balanced their allegiance between the two "superpowers." Intellectually too, the conflict helped thinkers in the Church and in the world to assert bold and original positions that incurred the hostility of either papacy or empire. The contemporary state also requires the presence of a strong spiritual authority, because a civilization that affirms its own aimlessness cannot long serve as the cement that holds society together.

The state, in its turn, tries to administer foolish remedies to secure a modicum of public peace, but since its ideology, whether liberal or socialist, is basically materialistic, it cannot, with the best effort of imagination, propose anything but public spending on mostly erroneously conceived projects. Its power today is largely, if not exclusively, money power, and is exerted in an endless round of raising tax money to spend on projects which multiply and require *more* money. Thus at the heart of state activities is a mechanism of two-way blackmail: pressure groups threaten the state with disruption of its circuits and the state threatens the citizens: if they do not pay, the public projects cannot continue. Is it not obvious that another institution is needed to break the vicious circle of spending to no purpose and to explain to society its real needs? Otherwise—that is, if the Church remains subservient to state-set social objectives—the much-vaunted separation of state and Church will become a sham: the state will move deeper into positions vacated by the Church and claim spiritual-moral direction over the citizens, in addition to its own legitimate powers. The "separation" will cease and the Church will again become an arm of the state.

Church intellectuals have indeed stated, following other ideologues, that religion is left with no other course in the welfare and the socialist state than to step aside in favor of the "civil religion," which does a better job of liquidating poverty and injustice. The Church itself in various countries (that is, the national conferences of bishops) has gone a long way toward believing this conclusion to be true and, confused about its identity and tasks, has all but consented to place the residue of its influence among the masses of believers in the service of the civic religion. But this is no service to state and society, which do not need another and another and another social agency; they need a spiritual and moral guide, as was emphasized by John Paul II during his visit to Mexico in 1979 and to other countries subsequently.

Moreover, in proportion as the Church has contented itself with its new role as a social agency, it has lost large numbers of the faithful, who did not go to church on Sunday to hear the "social gospel" expounded from the pulpit but to listen to spiritual words, conveying the good news of resurrection and eternal life. The irony, then, is that the tacit alliance between a confusedly acting state and a confusedly believing Church has not brought even the expected results. By preaching the social gospel of the tutelary state, the Church is making itself expendable. The decrease in its numbers and influence has turned it into a useless ally for the state, and possibly a moral burden for society.

The liberal-democratic-social welfare state is a neo-pagan state, even by its own admission, as its ideologues openly boast while they propose more desacralization and secularization. In the end, such a trend would undermine the state itself, which cannot exist and fulfill its functions unless the sacred is embedded in it. But the blind ideologues who push the state along this road are not aware of this. The Church, however, would fail in its vocation if it became similarly unaware that it deals with a new version of the pagan state and a never-yet-seen entity, a completely secularized society. Its tasks and duties are thus multiple and heavy, especially as (at present) it tries to help only those whom the state and its public philosophy designate as "victims" in need of assistance. But those whom the state takes under its tutelary wings are, alas, very often false or pseudo victims, and they wield political power. The state extends "protection" to them (in the form of legislation that favors, say, homosexuals or unwed mothers) because it fears their blackmail. Those whom the state does not protect (for example, victims of crime), since they cannot exert political pressure, are the real needy, and worthy of Church protection, even if it does not bring the Church public recognition. Public recognition, in the present circumstances, may be the sign of work *not* done.

One may have doubts about the value of spending untold millions for the supposed relief of such problems as crime, drugs, teen-age pregnancy, child abuse, alcoholism, and so on. These doubts are justified because the state does not spend these millions simply because this appears to be the most obvious thing to do in a rich country; it does so because its ideology offers the state no other perspective, no other option. Certain people may be tempted to say simply that many projects (like the one in New Jersey, designed to change sex attitudes) are thought up by idle minds, but this is not true. Behind such projects is the ideological will to effect not merely social changes but changes, first, in the human condition and then in the structure of man's mind and soul. There are many more projects on the agenda of this ideology. Abolition of the relationship between crime and punishment, by declaring crime to be a product of socio-economic disadvantage and the resulting warped psyche. Hence courts, police, and prisons are declared no barriers to crime, but new curricula in schools, taught by "reconditioned" teachers (who have learned to play a "managerial role in the classroom," as suggested by the New Jersey experiment), reduction of parents' traditional rights, and clinics and other "rehabilitation" centers. Another ideology-inspired project is "reformed think-ing" on drugs: legalization of some and nonpenalization for the use of nonlegalized drugs, and of course endless rehabilitation. Teen-age sex is another project: if not its outright encourage-ment, at least limitless indulgence, since, like "trial marriage," etc., it serves as a "pioneer case" for the transformation of sexual mores and, ultimately, liquidation of the family, drowned in indiscriminate sexual practices. "Gay rights": discreditation of sane sex instincts, the final objective of which is procreation, and their dissolution in a directionless mixity, with the cult of sheer animal pleasure as the final objective. The project to have Nobel-prize winners, presumably brilliant men, donate semen to produce brilliant offspring. These are only a few examples; un-fortunately, many more could be adduced.

It is hard to tell how much of this is anonymously spawned by our absurdist civilization, how much is hatched by intellectuals and ideologues, and how much is deliberately planned by gov-ernment and other bureaucrats. At any rate, the Church must condemn these plans and practices unequivocally, and engage in struggle against them by proclaiming that its aim is the saving of souls. As it is, the Church's voice, too often uncertain, even op-portunistic, inasmuch as it flatters the secular powers (whether actual or emerging), is at best corrective, and thus only one of many voices in the air around us. It ought to be the most re-sounding voice in defense of the stable elements and practices of society, a better civilization, a more righteous state. If the Church does not offer strong guidance to public morality, who will? And offer it not as social agencies do but as the source of moral knowledge and the depository of truth.

Thus we come to the issue of modern civilization as seen from the perspective of the Church. Our ears are full of the claim, intended to neutralize the Church's spiritual and magisterial power, that religion is only one of many trends in a pluralistic civilization, a trend of equal authority with all others. This claim is not just a strategy, it is the modern dogma; the highest verity is not this thing or another, it is the *multiplicity* of trends, all competing, like brand-name merchandise, for consumers' attention. The only truth is that there is no truth, only competing, equal options. Nevertheless, like some of the animals in Orwell's *Animal Farm,* some options are advertised as "more equal" than others, namely those which conform to the ideology of nontruth.

Who better than churchmen ought to see through this sham, even though it appears in the tranquillizing aspect of "neutrality" and "pluralism"? The Church, with unerring wisdom, has through the ages identified the enemies of civilization, not of this or that civilization but the enemies of moral principles that inform *all* civilizations. It combated paganism and the seductive heresies which were sophisticated amalgams of Gnostic, Manichaean, and Orphic doctrines; it resisted Averroist philosophy, which reduced faith to fideism and deprived it of the support of reason; it fought the Albigensians, with their liquidation of society and institutional relationships; it contradicted Enlightenment bred liberalism (with the *Syllabus of Errors* and the sermons of Cardinal Newman), Modernism (with Piux X's *Pascendi*), and contemporary totalitarianism (with *Divini Redemptoris* and *Mit Brennender Sorge*).

I have listed only a very few cases, but they show the nature of the Church's mission. Christian civilization is based on the universal understanding of things divine and human and, therefore, a universal response to human aspirations. It has a *timeless* aspect, to be gathered from Church pronouncements[27] and the moral shaping of society, and a *time-bound* aspect, like the art that grew, in extraordinary diversity, in the Church's civilizational concern. All this amounts to the proposition that reasserted Christian civilization should not be regarded as one modest current, paralleling others, but as the only real competitor of the civic religion.

This is not a self-seeking attitude of the Church; it affects, in the short and the long run, society and the state, helping them consolidate themselves and fulfill the tasks for which they were created. Put otherwise, the state and society need the church and can function only when civilization, which is their enveloping milieu, is permeated by religion. On the other hand, the Church needs the state. In the medieval nomenclature, the Church was the "soul," the state the "body," suggesting that they are inseparable. The Church assured the *felici tas aeterna,* the State was in charge of the *tranquillitas temporalis.* This is not different today, but words have changed; the area of civil society extends further now than in the past, and so does the area that is open to the state's intervention. This *laicization* of public life (as opposed to the imposition of the secular ideology) is not regrettable, it merely redistributes some functions and calls forth new competences.

The Christian is involved in areas where even the most dynamic Church policy should not reach (bearing in mind that the state too has a divinely appointed place in the life of men). The functions of the state are not to be regarded as superfluous after the Church has performed the vital functions; it tends the area where similarly vital functions are performed and come to fruition. It does not just relieve the Church of certain duties, it is the instigator of sovereign acts in its own right. The Church without the state would be a disincarnate community, tempted by theocratic rule. For its own good, the Church needs to be complemented by the state, and therefore must respect it. On the other hand, the state without the Church is a soulless monster and, in its own way, a "lay theocracy," in other words a totalitarian construct.

In a way, both institutions work with the same material: human beings and the communities they form. Do they have to make a choice between them? Do Church and state deal in the same manner with the individual and with society?

Clearly, the Church was instituted to save individual souls, and in this God-ordained approach it is at the antipode from contemporary ideologies which think in terms of masses and collectivism. Whether in Cuba or Cambodia, this ideology counts human beings in large blocs, decreeing that whole generations or entire nations and classes be sacrificed for the splendors of a hypothetical future. Individuals do not count, nor years, decades, or centuries, until a nebulous final goal is reached. In contrast, the Church is accountable for every head, here and now, since the worth of every soul is the same.

Moreover, while ideology is profoundly selfish insofar as it builds only what the Party, which incarnates it, says is essential, and neglects everything that is not in the Party's momentary interest (rapid industrialization, the whole population ordered to the rice fields, guns not butter), religion is a truly civilizing force; it builds, embellishes, inspires all things at the same time. Cathedrals have no priority over guilds, schools over hospitals, scholarship over missionary work. Religion inspires and enriches an entire civilization; ideology truncates and smothers even what exists. The Church is thus a corporation that consists of smaller corporations, wholly rooted in the present because the Church sets eyes on eternal truths at the intersection of the divine and the human.

This corporate nature is part of the essence of the Catholic religion and it is made evident in the Church's structure, where everybody fills a definite function. It has been said in recent times (but it is an old reproach) that the Church is "made for priests," that it is primarily a clerical institution in which lay believers are only "foot soldiers." Theologians like Hans Küng go so far as to deny the authenticity of Christ's words entrusting Peter with tending the flock. Küng's Protestant-inspired democratism (he acknowledges his great debt to Karl Barth, the Calvinist theologian) insists on abolition of the hierarchy for the supposed benefit of the "priestly people," as he calls Christian believers. Such views are superficial; they oppose the nature of community, which can persist only in a structured form. The Church's corporate nature is evident in its liturgy, in the celibacy of its priests (who as heads of families would pull apart and banalize the corporation), in its pyramidal structure, and in the infallibility of the pope. All of these constituting elements enable the Church to move as one body, and also, sure of its unity, to ensure the widest diversity of positions.

Yet this corporate nature does not contradict the fact that, by the teaching of its Founder, the Church really "pulls" in the direction of the individual, the human person. Incarnation is an individual act; Christ became *one* man, born in a certain environment, with parents, an occupation, a personality; he did not become mankind or a group. Apart from his divine nature, he had, as a man, a distinct personality, preferences, a personal history, clear physical and psychological outlines. The Church is forever marked by this personality, and also by Christ's first commandment, summed up as "What you do to the smallest among men you are doing to me." This stress on the individual is also seen in the actions of saints and mystics. Whether founders of orders or contemplators, they insist that even in the *unio mystica* man remains a separate personality, just as he remains a distinct individual in monastery and convent, where he is known and treated as such by his superiors. A Mother Teresa does not deal with social classes and ideological blocks, the objects of her charity are individuals in need to know, once in their life, that they can be loved and cared for in God's name.

The vocation of the *state* is different; it "pulls" in the direction of the community. The believer's soul is to be saved; the citizen's soul is not the state's primary concern. Its primary concern is the coordinated conduct of all citizens—clearly an issue where the community, in this case the nation, takes precedence over its individual component parts. It is, naturally, the citizen who must be protected, whose well-being must be assured, whose rights must be observed. But basically the citizen seeks his own individual objectives; he forms associations to promote them in the company of other individuals who seek similar aims. He does not have to be protected in every way, his natural inclinations are in most respects sufficient, whereas, in comparison with what happens in the spiritual order, his own efforts are not adequate for the salvation of his soul.

Those who argue for the citizen's protection by the state in every endeavor forget that the price of such protection is that ultimately, the state will assign his endeavors. They also ignore the wisdom of the principle of subsidiarity, according to which all human activities should be directed and corrected at the lowest rung of social bodies where this is feasible, so that every problem may find its remedy by the competence of those who are immediately involved.

When we say that by its nature the state "pulls" toward the community, we mean that its primary task is to supervise the collective functioning of society, to make sure that the collectivity functions as such. In most of these dealings, individuals are in some form of conflict with the community, and the state must be wise enough to know that the common interest must prevail over the individual interest, that in limited cases the law that protects the first has precedence over that which protects the second. In our falsely individualistic times ("falsely" because not individuals but aggressive pressure groups are in fact protected, to which the individual may then belong), we have all but forgotten the language of the common good. Does the contract theory, so popular in our midst, not tell us that the individual's right is more important than the right of the community?

Solzhenitsyn reminded us of the correct perspective when he pointed out, in his speech at Harvard (and on other occasions), that courts and the media (the two dictating powers of the "new democracy") insist on the sacredness of the individual right and depreciate the national interest. Indeed, the legal nexus and the First Amendment are utilized as fetishes, at the expense of ordinary decency and national interest, and the latter is not even understood while the exclusive sacredness of individual rights is extolled. (We remember the judge who found against the government in the Ellsberg Case and stated that the national interest [in this instance, defense secrets] has no priority over the right of the individual to disclose and make public these secrets.)

These instances show the weakness of the state, which is today confused about its function as protector of the community. We said before that the contemporary ideology conducts radical attacks against all institutions, not merely in order to demolish them but especially to demonstrate that institutions are congealed "class interests," hiding their violent repressiveness behind some respectable façade. The primary target of such attacks used to be the Church ("The believer needs no sacraments, clergy, imposed morality, magisterium"); now it is the state ("Individuals can police themselves and live together according to their fraternal impulses"). No wonder that the state is confused about its identity and usurps too many functions, while it neglects the functions which belong to its essence.

Any individual may bring suit against the state, which the Old Testament approved when the king expropriated the poor man's house and vineyard. But at present, contrary excesses are noted: the state often remains practically defenseless when its protective branches are under attack by ex-officials' disclosure of secret operations or by congressional committees' demand that such operations (for example, intelligence gathering) be conducted in the open or not at all. The principle of hierarchy is replaced by the new principle of "codetermination," which has been propagated in the permissive family, the progressive classroom, and the collectively run factory, and is now extended to the state itself, which is supposed to share its customary attributes with the totality of citizens. (At the beginning of this century, a French Christian Democrat actually suggested the formula: "Government of everybody by everybody.") Again Solzhenitsyn may be quoted:

> A society without any objective legal scale is a terrible one, indeed. But a society with no other scale but the legal one is not quite worthy of man either.... Wherever the tissue of life is woven of legalistic relations, there is an atmosphere of moral mediocrity, paralyzing man's noblest impulses.

Let us draw conclusions from our reflections.

Church and state need each other, for the good life of the individual and society that both supply by means of integrity and progress.

The Church leans in the direction of the individual person, with his unique and uniquely valuable soul; the state leans in the direction of the community as guarantor of the public good (*res publica utilitatis communio*).

Neither neglects the aspect which is second on its agenda: the Church is a corporation, and the state upholds the citizen's rights through its laws.

This preestablished harmony of state and Church is the foundation of what we call Christian order and civilization.

Chapter 5
The Problems of the Present

The relationship of Church and state is not abstract; it is crucial and concrete, and concretely different in each historical time, varying according to countries and conditions. Our general statement about this relationship, which is valid under all circumstances, is obtained from Etienne Gilson: The Church is both involved in and aloof from *politics:* the first, because the Church cannot remain indifferent to what happens in the multiple spheres of morals and social actions; the second because, as a *sui generis* corporation and as Christ's representative, it does not participate in the daily concerns and movements in political, economic, and cultural transactions.

This fact at once raises the question of the diversity of regimes which operate at any time, influencing generations and events. If, as just stated, the Church is preoccupied indirectly, that is, through its concern for men's moral welfare, with the politics of nations and the form of the state, it is inevitable that it behave differently in regard to every community and every period. Two truths are juxtaposed here, but it would be an error to suggest that they are contradictory. One is the Church's stand that it favors no regime as following from its doctrine: the Church's understanding of politics is such that in its eyes the citizens, tradition, circumstances, the slow shifts of history, etc., determine the form of a regime—not a particular affirmative or negative statement by Church authorities or even authoritative and endorsed works by Church doctors. The other truth is that, given the nature of the regime, a specific range of problems arises, in regard to which Catholic teaching takes a certain position.

The delicate balance between these "two truths," as we may call them, may not be easy to maintain in given circumstances, when, without doctrine-inspired prudence, grave problems that arise in a regime would tempt the Church to recommend that the regime be changed. Yet such is not the Church's task; thus the two truths remain compatible: whatever the regime, the Church must work within it, and always for its improvement. There is room in Catholic thought for the greatest variety of political forms that mankind has conceived or will conceive (except, of course, regimes that base their central thrust on immoral or life-denying principles)—from pagan to religion-inspired forms—yet, whatever the form, the Church owes it to Christ to denounce injustice, immorality, lack of elementary freedom, and other acts which implicitly negate man's spiritual and social nature.

In concrete circumstances, the church is confronted, as an institution and as the moral protector of believers, with questions about the role of authority, the nature of democracy, plurality, justice, the distribution of power and prosperity, etc., in a given state. Catholic intellectuals are far from thinking uniformly; they read the history of their nations and that of the human race in various lights and reach different answers, though more or less all of them are in apparent conformity with Christian truth.

The nineteenth-century Italian thinker Taparelli, who was very influential for a time, fashioned the function of authority in the state on the model of Christ's authority in the Church. The latter was made visible through the Incarnation, and it was Taparelli's view that the state too should be a strongly visible arbiter among the various groups; otherwise their conflicts would bring society to chaos. Another view emanates from Pius X, expressed in an encyclical, and in a way, it took sides in the controversy about equality in a Christian society. The Church, the pope wrote in 1906, is an unequal society, where some teach, guide and judge; others obey and follow, and thus are led to the Christian objectives for which the Church was founded. A third case (to limit the number of illustrations) is that of Fr. John Courtney Murray, in whose view a tradition exists in the United States according to which Catholics find in American civil society a near ideal situation, allowing all men to practice their beliefs freely, just as they freely engage in their other interests and enterprises. The American Jesuit denied the state the right to enforce any religious faith, arguing that this was perhaps desirable in conflict-torn Europe but not in this country, where social mores are such that, within a very wide framework, Church, society, and state can comfortably coexist.

If we look closely at these three positions, we find only differences of emphasis, and perhaps (here and there) historical shortsightedness. Taparelli did not propose that the state legislate religious and spiritual matters; Pius X spoke only of inequality in the Church, not in civil society; and John Courtney Murray put his trust in the pluralistic society, not in a "balance" maintained by the state. In his advocacy of state authority, Taparelli may have been influenced by the need of the nascent Italian monarchy to pull together the regional autonomies which even today, more than a century later, contribute to the near anarchical conditions of the peninsula. In his advocacy of social pluralism, Murray had not yet fully experienced the rise in America of a tutelary state which would legislate against Catholic moral doctrine in sexual and family matters. Pope Pius X was not influenced by concrete contingencies when he asserted that the Church—he explicitly referred to the "Mystical Body of Christ"—does not constitute a community of equals; nor would he have been in error if he had drawn the implicit conclusion that civil society too is a body of unequal men and women, where the natural law of the division of functions operates for the good of all.

It is natural that in this chapter we will look at the relationship between Catholics and the state in America, and it is equally natural (as well as prudent) to look at it in the light of other historical situations also, since we have just seen to what extent specific local circumstances may influence the views of even outstanding thinkers.

Fr. Murray's general perspective leads us to the heart of the matter. His conviction that Catholics, together with other citizens in the past, present, and future, "hold these truths"[1] (those expressed in the founding documents) to be self-evident, indicates that he saw, like many other Americans, a historic break in the annals of Western men: despotic and anarchistic Europe on one side and the United States on the other, the latter exemplifying mankind's aspiration for a harmonious relationship between the government and the governed. He saw the original contribution of the United States, again like most other Americans, in the preponderance of civil society over the state, and he saw the common good as the result less of government action than of a happy consensus of the citizens, even when it arises from their myriad (but not irreconcilable) conflicts.[2]

It is interesting to note, however, that the perspective (may we say the *Catholic* perspective?) has changed drastically between 1960, the year in which *We Hold These Truths* was published, and 1978, the date of appearance, in the more modest format of a brochure, of *The Present Position of Catholics in America,* by Professor James Hitchcock.[3] The change, from complete and lighthearted optimism to alarmed pessimism has more than just an American significance; it has, indeed, the significance of a paradigm for contemporary developments.

In many parts of the Catholic world it is now sensed, even if not yet perfectly understood (let alone acted upon), that Catholics today face a different kind of danger than in the past. We marshaled arguments in this respect in the preceding chapter and it is worth repeating them here: In the past, Catholics, standing solidly in the Church, confronted one rival which was often (though not always) hostile: the state. The penetration of Christian moral, social, and esthetic principles in society was sufficient for resisting the state, which, it must be said, was likewise permeated by these principles. Thus one could speak of rivalry rather than clearcut enmity. At present, however, Christians confront not merely a completely secular state but a desacralized, pagan society as well, whose impact on the state desacralizes the latter even more than would otherwise be the case. For in democratic regimes the state is bound to respond to, and indeed reflect, the manifest trends in the social body, so that the reciprocal relationship between civil society and the state irresistibly promotes the paganization of both, affecting in the process the thinking of many churchmen, if not indeed the very structure of the Church, in a manner that must also be labeled "desacralizing." Wherever the process started, the fact is that state and society, and the often vacillating and ambiguously behaving Church, are practically engulfed by a neo-pagan ideology, leaving Catholics, used to corporate living and corporate responses, alone and isolated in a new and confusing situation.

At the level of concrete observations, Hitchcock's booklet documents this shift, which took place between 1960 (before the Council) and 1978, well in the postconciliar times of trials and tribulations. The author remains within the American perspective, as his title suggests, and his diagnosis takes less in consideration the "Council and after" than the watershed which, in his judgment, the presidency of John F. Kennedy represented from the point of view of the evolution of American Catholicism. Briefly, his thesis is that American Catholics were so impressed by the election of "one of theirs" to the highest office that they began, for the first time, to feel completely integrated with their country, whose basic principles they have therefore unquestionably and uncritically adopted. But, Hitchcock argues—and the difference with John Courtney Murray is striking—since these basic principles are often inimical to the Catholic concept of truth, morals, and even politics, the newly accented integral citizenship in fact "de-Catholicizes" Catholic citizens. In short, they accept, approve, and vote and work for laws, measures, and policies that, twenty years ago, they would have indignantly rejected.[4]

Hitchcock speaks of the "decline of the public influence of the Catholic community," which leaves unchallenged those "influential elements in American society—in academe, the media, government agencies, and in the courts—who have embarked on a brilliantly successful strategy to secularize the nation in a systematic way." As we have done (in this and other works),[5] the author identifies the doctrine which inspires this secularization with the "humanistic religion," the more pernicious as it is not publicly recognized as a religion, thus exempt from the guidelines of the separation of state and Church. Humanism, the creed of the intellectual elite, has thus all the advantages work for it, while the resistance it meets is mostly passive, sporadic, and fast deflected from its course by the refusal of the universities and the media to give it their attention.

It may be regarded as unfortunate that, after writing a courageous and truthful essay, Professor Hitchcock recommends paltry remedies for radical evils. The remedies concern mostly a switching of Catholic voting patterns, closer scrutiny of political candidates, and ecumenical efforts to bring pressure on federal and state legislatures. The author, a professor of history, ought to know that an ideological tidal wave cannot be stopped and reversed by voting for this or that candidate or by waiting for the passing of more favorable laws.

On these pages we do not propose programs for action; we merely elaborate the Catholic perspective, first of all keeping in mind the permanent necessity that Catholics judge the "political thing"—whether or not action follows—in the light of the Church's traditional teaching.

The fashionable belief today is that state and society have nothing more to learn from religion and the Church. Such a belief is characteristic of ages in which social and political forms have entered their period of decline, although to sophisticated contemporaries it appears that these forms had reached their apogee. Individualism, in such periods, is so absolute that people are convinced of the unique value of their own way of life and thinking; these little, self-contained universes proclaim they do not need institutions, particularly those which are old and have a moral message. Liberal and socialist partisans of the two leading ideologies believe they stand above institutions which embody the lessons of history and claim to "know better" than the individual. *Liberals* are convinced of these things because the producer—consumer society has brought them unprecedented well-being, a state of affairs they translate as the terminus of history, the point of perfection which gives sense to the human race in time, an otherwise meaningless process. The "invisible hand" or the "clash of atoms" (or whatever else is behind this process) follows its course anyway; all that the individual must do is to seek his personal happiness in this flux. As Cardinal Newman wrote, the principle of the liberal attitude is that whether we find or lose a fragile and questionable "truth" has no importance: opinions are there to be accepted or rejected; belief is a matter of reason, it commits us to nothing; it should not be allowed to permeate our being; in all matters, the self is the sole judge, and thus there is no need of an external guide.[6]

The *socialist* also believes in his independence of institutions and their teaching. Institutions belong to the "dark ages" of the human chronicle, when they embodied, under various façades, the class interests of the powerholders and repressed the aspirations of the poor. In the coming world, they will be swept away by equal ownership of the means of production, when there will be no powerful and powerless. The few things that institutions justifiably preserved, beautiful art and the culture compressed in books—in other words, institutions like museums, libraries, and schools—will be the dis-institutionalized property of the collectivity in which all will participate, according to their personal tastes and inclinations.

All these ideal features, which constitute not so much the ideology as the *mythology* of our times, whether of liberals or socialists, are antihistorical and antimoral, and they plunge men into an increasingly uncertain present and future. Since, in spite of the "revolutionary times" in which we live, the flow of generations cannot but be gradual; traditional attitudes still pierce the veil of modernity at many places, so that we hardly notice the move away from our anchored position. Thus in the last century a Taine or a Renan, harshly rationalistic and antireligious, admitted in their mature years that their moral code (their attitude toward life, private convictions, even their scholarly integrity) had been warmed by the theology they learned in their youth, without which this moral code cools and can no longer sustain itself by its own energy. But a time comes when the earlier warmth of truth, its flames no longer fanned, is only a cold memory in books of scholarship; the state and the society, then, lose the spiritual-moral content that religion alone can supply. Certain individuals or groups may retain a living relationship with this vital substance, but cold times come upon a society when such a relationship is no longer assured through the channel of institutions and when these channels transmit only empty, verbal currents.

This is where Western mankind now stands. The prodigious growth of society and state (the liberal as well as the socialist state) has muffled the spiritual voice of religion, to such an extent that it has also shaken the faith of the Church in its own mission and has prompted churchmen to speak a despiritualized and amoral language, that of liberals and socialists, that of state and society. To use the language of the fashionable research into ancestral Indo-European tribal life, of the three functions, each fulfilled by a category of men: prayer, war, and work (or God, nation, and agriculture/industry)—one function, that of the priests, has become as if paralyzed. The "activist" principles are overgrown; the spiritual, which ought to motivate the other principles, has been thinned out.

Even a so-called conservative prelate, Italian Cardinal Colombo, recently said about Church–state relationships: Genuine freedom should prevail in modern society; we want no privileges for the Church. The state should have a "healthy lay character" and "ethical principles," without which man lacks dignity.[7]

But the cardinal ignores several points. Where should the "ethical principles" be derived, if, as Taine and Renan learned too late, the glow of Christian teaching has no more warmth to generate and sustain them? And though the "lay character" of the state is not questioned in Catholic doctrine, are we so sure that it remains "healthy" under the powerful impact of modern ideology, whether capitalism, Marxism, socialism, or technocracy?

"Pluralism" is often a false label, under which it simply is not true that "all opinions have an equal chance of expressing themselves and being heard." It can fast degenerate into a vehicle for a particular ideology and can promote its cause through privileged means, until it reaches a virtual monopoly position. To put it bluntly, if, among all "competing opinions" the Church's does not enjoy certain "privileges," the result will not be a status of equality for all points of view but the privileged position of an anti-Church opinion. Communities cannot long exist without a central belief, which is produced by the mere fact that human beings gather and view their gathering as possessing symbolic significance. If this central belief is not Christian (in the West), it can only be anti-Christian. There is no escape from the horns of dilemma.

This problematic brings us back to the American situation. Catholics have long assumed (the culminating point of their assumption is incorporated in Fr. Murray's book)[8] that they have the qualified status of tolerated citizens, incompletely integrated due to their political shortcomings; and this feeling can be historically explained. The United States was a Protestant foundation, and has been a Protestant country with a Protestant public philosophy, which peaks in the famous "consensus," or, to put it with more articulation, in a policy that is based on the "deliberate sense of the people." Catholics, as such, did not participate in the founding of the Republic and did not contribute to the formulation of the founding documents. The majority of them came to this country later, as immigrants—as poor or impoverished immigrants to a country where Protestant values justified the accumulation of wealth. Moreover, these Catholics came from countries where the very opposite of a consensus had prevailed for long centuries, which were torn (for the same number of centuries) by conflicts between state, Church, nobility, burghers, corporations, intellectuals, and social classes. Catholic immigrants' awe before the American consensus and its favorable economic consequences are understandable. They felt tolerated. A further step was acceptance; the final step, assimilation. The crowning (or apotheosis?) was Kennedy's presidency.

This success story, or, if you wish, this blessed marriage between Catholics and America, should not hide from our eyes the nature of the Republic.[9] As Walter Berns puts it, from the beginning the United States was destined to be a large, commercial commonwealth, with great emphasis on material goods, produced and consumed, and a corresponding deemphasis of moral underpinnings.[10] More than that, this commonwealth has demonstrated its durability (historical contingencies such as hugeness and isolation helped too, of course) and has become one of the rare lands in the West and in the world which has not changed regimes, constitutions, or its basic system of belief during its two centuries' existence. Thus to criticize the American system is one thing; to refer to another model in this criticism is another. No such model exists in the American experience and, hence, in the mentality of Americans.

The emphasis on material goods and the pursuit of happiness, as mentioned by Professor Berns, in itself is enough to create a certain feeling of alienation in Catholics vis-à-vis America—not disloyalty (let us hasten to add), not the reversal of constructive assimilation, but a critical stance, a certain detachment from some aspects of American life—let us say in the manner of an H. L. Mencken. This, however, seems impossible: the more the Catholic community became an integral part of the nation—and the process is obviously completed—the less it was able to *imagine* any political and social forms other than the historically American forms. This is understandable, we argued, due to Catholics' unsatisfactory background in Europe and to the full satisfaction that their non-Catholic fellow citizens feel vis-à-vis the Constitution, the national way of life, the American form of government. But it is less understandable if we look at the *Catholic* background of these Catholics, the Catholic doctrine and culture, which ought to play an influential role in these matters.

It can be plausibly argued that those whom Professor Willmoore Kendall labeled as at least latent enemies of the "consensus," namely, the recently emerged but by now established bureaucrats and auxiliary intellectuals, who advocate and impose "theoretical absolutes," are not people who dropped from the sky but simply *radical* interpreters of American liberal-democratic ideology and, therfore, continuators of certain trends on which the nation was founded. The permissive, ultraliberal, even antinational elements—the academics, the media people, the government bureaucrats, etc., whom Professor Hitchcock mentions—are not necessarily carriers of an alien point of view; they elaborate and impose modes of thought, that are embedded in the American theory of a happy society. As Leo Strauss wrote, these people, in one word the "intelligentsia," are not diabolical; they simply "reflect the most dangerous proclivities of democracy."[11]

Strauss's conclusion is that liberal democracy does not seem able to defend itself against such elements, partly because it has a built-in tendency for excess, partly because it knows no principle which would allow it to demote its domestic adversaries from positions of power and influence. This Straussian analysis is shared by a number of American political thinkers, but as we saw in the case of Hitchcock, none is able to go beyond the analysis and its negative conclusions. Either political imagination or political courage is lacking.

One logical and natural assumption would be to expect Catholic political men and intellectuals to take the initiative of breaking out of the magic circle. If the Protestant concept of state and society has been to a certain extent alien to them, how much more is its radicalized excrescence, the amalgam of immorality, permissiveness, antipatriotism, family destruction, etc., which now emanates from such vital centers as universities, the media, the courts, state legislatures, Congress, government departments (like HEW), or institutional lobbies (like NEA)? It is evident that the combined effect of these influences today defines the public attitude and public policy. One might even argue that America's Catholics would best show their gratefulness for complete assimilation by attempting to save the nation and its foundation principles from this kind of decrepitude and decay.

No such signs can be detected. "Consensus," and whatever can be subsumed under this heading, hypnotize American Catholics, to such an extent that they do not distinguish between the old consensual society and the new, between the legitimate and the illegitimate. Of course, they share this feeling with perhaps the majority of their fellow citizens, and together they believe that whatever remains of the old principles is still a reliable rampart against the "theoretical absolutes" which have come to dominate public and private existence. The question is only one of metaphor: Are these principles still a *rampart* or are they a *raft*, floating uncertainly on raging, hostile waters?

Let us admit, however, that the problem is not so simple and that America's Catholics are understandably puzzled. Could they make a united stand today under the Church's guidance? A delicate and fluid interrogation that nobody seems anxious to ask or answer. We have argued on these pages that no society can last without a religious faith, embedded at its core and influencing the moral and social milieu. But we have also pointed out that, in the changed circumstances of this century, the formidable new powers of society and state (both desacralized!) have had a nefarious impact on the churches too, in some cases actually desacralizing them, in other cases weakening their sense of truth, with a consequent alteration of their sense of mission. Let us therefore ask quite brutally: Can the Church be relied upon to help reinvigorate the social fabric, to detach itself sufficiently from its admiration of, and often its servility to, the public ideology of neo-paganism?

Last century's great Russian religious philosopher, V. Soloviov, ever on the threshold of conversion to Catholicism, reproached the Church for having stressed, throughout history, the *human* element in the Incarnation. The consequence was an exaggerated admiration for the human being, his reason, his rights, his power. Soloviov was by no means entirely wrong; the Church, in spite of the wise, measured, and balanced statements of popes and doctors, has contributed to the development of rationalistic philosophy and, even more certainly, the elaboration of humanism. Today we reap the consequences in the temporal order and their repercussions in the spiritual order, in the very life of the Church.

So the question remains: Can the Church be counted upon to reinstill its wisdom into the public philosophy? Professor Hitchcock's brochure lists a painful number of cases, from educational matters to abortion, where the bishops have yielded (we speak here of the post-Kennedy, post–Vatican II era) to secular pressure, even to secularistic principles. Such nonresistance could be documented in other countries also.

Let us carefully distinguish two propositions, two attitudes, in this respect.

a) Throughout its long existence, the Church has been a master in the art of reconciling divine wisdom and human prudence. It has always moved slowly and circumspectly on the turbulent waters of human affairs, and *adapted itself to circumstances when these circumstances became mature enough to adapt themselves to the Church's wisdom.* This is, I think, the essence of the relationship between Church and society, Church and state, Church and ideology, Church and the forces outside it. To speak of the present, this is obvious today in the Vatican's *Ostpolitik,* and also in the election of a Polish pope. In this connection, it can be said that we are witnessing the initial phases of the Church's move in the direction of the "modern worldview" (*not* "modernist"), a term we use for lack of a better one.

There is no reason to be alarmed by this move; in his work on the development of doctrine, Newman has magisterially unraveled as well as justified the process. There is no reason to be alarmed by it, that is, if the doctrinal position remains stable and fully asserted and practice is not modified but, let us say, "enlarged," so as to embrace the new circumstances. John Paul II did just this in his Mexican and Brazilian discourses and again in his first encyclical, *Redemptor Hominis.* He spoke, for example, of the "social responsibility of property," which is not by any means a novelty in pontifical literature over the centuries, but is seemingly new in the circumstances in which the pope used the words. He took note of the pressures in this direction which emanate from socialist forces and from the loud South American partisans of "liberation theology." Accordingly, his expression was: "Every private property is socially mortgaged." The phrase should be read in the context of the radical declaration by the bishop of Cuernavaca, Mendez Arceo,[12] or the moderate but "progressive" article of Matagrin, bishop of Grenoble.[13]

b) The second proposition and attitude has to do with principles that are rooted in doctrine, and possibly go even deeper. A good number of official documents—episcopal, theological, pastoral, synodal—indicate that at least some segments of the Church have engaged on a subtle redefinition of the God-to-man relationship. Starting from apostolic affirmations that "God is love," they interpret "love" to mean what contemporary intellectual fashion happens to dictate: social concern, carefree happiness, human self-satisfaction, and, if necessary, revolution and the totalitarian state. Even if we take only the more anodyne expressions as the prevailing view in some sectors of Church thinking, namely, that God shows his love of man by not inflicting pain and punishment and by showing infinite indulgence toward sin and aberration, we may note that such an "all sweetness" conception of God does not conform to the scriptural view. Indeed, between the lines of effusion about this God, who like an older companion or a good daddy shuts his eyes on the "modern lifestyle," one can read both a *liberal*-Protestant attitude of indifferentism and a revolutionary-Marxist analysis of the social structure.

The first, because when one denies the distance between God and man, the motivation is to aggrandize man at God's expense. The notion of an all-forgiving and generously "understanding" God suggests that man is master and judge of his actions, that no higher reference exists. The second, because when our contemporaries fashion a God who is an all-sweetness-and-love figure, they mean that history has "moved forward"; modern man no longer sees God as a severe father but as a fraternal guide. This transformation is then interpreted as a result of structural changes in society: the old society was repressive, *therefore* it imagined God as a harsh ruler; because the new society is "brotherly," it needs a democratically governing God. In one and the other instance, God is made irrelevant; he is banalized—a pale figure who automatically approves and applauds modern man. Such a God is hardly more than a human artifact.

Such is the case at present, in our estimation. Its overall meaning is that Catholics (American and most other) find themselves in a perplexing, even painful situation. On one hand there is the imperative need to resist the state and society, which are luxuriating in a desacralized climate and have adopted the ideology of secular humanism as the only one that corresponds to the aspirations of modern, rational, liberated man. On the other hand, there are the equally desacralized sectors of the clergy who also subscribe in all but name (?) to the tenets of secular humanism[14] and try to turn the Church into a propaganda agency for godless regimes, be they liberal or Marxist. The question is, once again, Can the Church be regarded as a motor force—or less, a guide, or at worst an auxiliary—in the struggle for a Christian civilization?

Thus we meet the essence of politics that Catholics should preeminently practice but also, before everything else, understand. Politics is, first of all, integrated with human nature; it follows from the social nature of man. Second, there are good and bad politics, the former consisting of appropriate means in reaching good objectives. Restoration of a Christian civilization is certainly the noblest objective imaginable; and "civilization" suggests an adequate restoration of state and society, which should (at least) be brought to conformity with Christian principles, even if Christian principles are not embedded in every document and action.

This general formulation of politics for our time includes an agenda and a timetable. The Catholic citizen must assert his beliefs on two fronts, the temporal and the spiritual. The novelty of the present situation is that he must be a political man, not only in the first but also in the second area. For Americans, this is particularly baffling and trying, since their Church, never as deeply involved in temporal politics as the Church in Europe and in South America, is now part of the political landscape. To make matters worse, the Church is an ambiguous part of this landscape; it does not quite know how to behave in its new role. To become *political* in the ecclesiastical realm does not mean that American Catholics be *politicized:* the stakes are higher than in temporal politics because not only the Church but the well-being of state and society depends on it, and to a considerable extent the salvation of souls.[15]

To sum up, the task of American Catholics is to penetrate the Church with a political sense—not only as parishioners, believers, communicants, disbursers of charity. When Vatican II invited ordinary Catholic laymen to participate (whatever the thrust of the invitation), the left wing took immediate advantage of the offer and the right wing adopted and accepted the position of a "remnant." This is self-defeating, paralyzing, and scandalous. The objective—internal restoration of the Church and resumption of its role as a moral guide of society—is so vital, spiritually so decisive, that it cannot be left to the bishops alone, and certainly not to the ecclesiastical bureaucracies. War is too important a matter, as the saying goes, to be left to the generals.

The understanding that politics, not in the sense of electing the local candidate to a county, state, or federal position, but in the wider sense of making long-range, statesmanlike moves, is essential today, but it does not come easily to Americans and thus to Catholic Americans, used to politicking on the ward level. Yet, aware of what is at stake, one must acquire the political art, as one acquires the art of navigation for the stormy sea.

For all the postconciliar rhetoric, the universal Church is not becoming more democratic in its structure; but in the spirit of modern times, the leaders invite the masses to a large participation. The Church, which is neither democratic nor theocratic, but on the level of the temporal is a true polity, should rejoice that its sons and daughters display the virtues of citizens within its fold.

What does it mean that (American) Catholics should penetrate the church with a political sense? It means three things:

1) Once in conversation with a dynamic Protestant pastor, I was told that these are trying but invigorating times because religious people may set out on their own to fight for Christian truth. I retorted that this may be true of Protestants with their individualistic approach to truth and doctrine, but not of Catholics who form a corporation, the Church. Only the Church as a whole, and then under the Pope's direction, can enter the battle for faith, doctrine, and civilization. A corporation, is, however, in many respects a political body, it must be organized, structured with institutions,[16] and its awareness is a collective awareness under the responsibility of those whose function it is to guide it. "Political sense" in the Church means then the reaffirmation that bishops, clergy, and theologians must provide moral and intellectual guidance according to the tenets of orthodoxy. To awaken their vocation that many of them have allowed to dissolve in the surrounding secularist ideologies is the equivalent of demanding that they perform their institutional duties; the (political) pressure on them to do so—the pressure by laymen on the hierarchy in view of saving drifting or derelict souls—is as legitimate as its civilian equivalents in the State.

Many Church historians distinguish in the Church a *descending* form of authority from an *ascending* form: authority exercised from above by popes, doctors, conciliar formulations, and from below, by laymen and lower clergy. We have in mind here the latter. To emphasize it, is neither conciliarism (the superiority of councils over popes), nor an effort to smuggle liberalism and democracy into the Church's structure; it is the recognition that the Church is also a *mixed polity* where the absence or negligence of the commanding echelons is repaired by the obeying ones—to use the earlier quoted terms of Pius X.

b) Such an action, such a pressure, can be justified when we remember that the Church is not only the Mystical Body or a pure phantasm—this is the view of John of Paris and to some extent of Luther—it is also an institution with a human face. Thus to argue that certain rules of politics apply to the Church is merely the acknowledgement of a fact. If Jesus had not held this view, he would not have entrusted the supreme guidance of the Church to Peter; he, Jesus, would have remained Himself an immanent force in the Church, guaranteeing an automatic perfection. Such an attitude on Christ's part would be a "Calvinistic" one: the Word of the Lord as flowing from the mouth of the elect would be the single crystalline gushing forth, next to which everything is a merely human, possibly devilish, invention.[17] It is evident that this is not the way the Church functions. It functions *politically* in the sense that it is immersed in the world, being sensitive, unlike Karl Barth, to everything happening in the world.

It is therefore not to diminish the Church's status to say that its vastness, complex structure, multiformity, historical traditions, and universal objectives—but of course mainly its central task to save souls, a task to which the others are subordinated—have made of the Church from the moment of its foundation (and not from Constantine) a *political body* in which the various parts entertain political relationships with each other. Internal pressure exercised in the cause of salvation does not profane the Church's sacred character. We may say, analogically, that just as Christ was not a dis-incarnate entity, the employment of human means in the Church is tolerable and natural.

c) The pontificate of John Paul II demonstrates, indeed, that the *sensus fidelium* has been in unison with the highest authority. The Pontif's actions vindicate the people's growing consternation

about the Church's domestic abuses: the impudence of theologians as they play with Gospel and doctrinal interpretations,
the clergy's contempt for their own status as mediators between
God and men, the bishops' dereliction of authority, and the
drifting of all three classes toward the cascading process of
secularization, politicisation, and radicalization. Formal apostasy
may or may not follow any one of these characteristic abuses.

If we hesitate to call the present pope's procedure political,
it is because public opinion does not usually associate the term
with the action of Church authority. Yet, it is clear that the
Pope's actions have a political facet: measures to secure the
tranquillitas which, in a way, is *temporalis,* even if the immediate
consequences—given the Church's otherworldly vocation—are
impacts on the *felicitas aeterna*.

Thus John Paul's actions appear as mandated by the people.
Does it mean that the people had been under obligation to wait
for the pope and his actions, that they would not have been—that
they were in fact not—justified to pressure the bad shepherds
without the signal from Rome? The answer is, I believe, that
John Paul's policies have not merely the effect of justifying and
legitimizing the people's earlier discontent, but that this discontent was justified and legitimate even if John Paul had not
undertaken the actions he actually has. Thus political pressure
on the bad shepherds would have been and was justified and
legitimate at the occasions they occured even before the present
pontificate. Not, let me emphasize, political pressure by manip-
ulating the secular representatives of the State and their voting
pattern, but domestic pressure on the clergy, hierarchy and
theologians.

It has happened before and it is a lesson for the future.

Notes

Introduction

1. Aptly did Solzhenitsyn comment on our age, remarking that one of the fundamental rights of men ought to be the right *not to be informed,* not to be bombarded by trivial, irrelevant, obsessive "facts," coercing him, in spite of his incompetence, to take part.

2. *L'Avenir radieux* (Lausanne: Ed. l'Age d'Homme, 1978).

3. My students display shock and unbelief when I tell them, for example, that Germany may one day be reunified, that military regimes are growing in number, that East Europeans regard Russia, Communist or not, as belonging to Asian civilization, etc.

4. Ta-ling Lee and Miriam London, "A Chinese Round Table on the Passing of Mao," *Freedom at Issue* (March/April 1977).

Chapter 1

1. Ruth Whitehouse, *The First Cities* (London: Phaidon/ Oxford, 1977).

2. L. Kolapowski, *Chrétiens saus Eglise,* Gallimard, 1969.

3. F. W. Walbank, *A Historical Commentary on Polybius,* Oxford, at Clarendon Press, 1957, p. 21.

4. *De Republica,* I, xxv, 39.

5. "The Church never ceased to teach that respect for authority is a religious duty, and she never hesitated to recognize any form of government, provided it guaranteed and respected the rights of God and Church." A. Passerin d'Entrèves, *La notion de l'Etat,* éd. Sirey, Paris, 1967, p. 276.

6. This does not mean that Catholic teaching has no criteria for the goodness or at least adequateness of political regimes. If Bishop Bossuet writes that all forms of government have their flaws, so that the best thing to do is remain in the one that time and habit have made familiar (*Politique tirée des propres paroles de l'Ecriture sainte*, p. 59 [II. XII]), this is not necessarily the common teaching. This teaching insists not on habit but on *legitimacy*, which also means wide acceptance by the people and conformity to laws, justice, and freedoms. Bossuet himself cites the Old Testament, which accepts the legitimacy of certain conquests and "peaceful possession [by the conquerors] of a territory for three hundred years."

7. Political kidnaping and assassination in this century have often been connected with the victim's "trial" before a "people's" or "workers'" tribunal. This, more than the acts of violence themselves, have represented a threat to state authority. Since the function of judging is a function of the state, the terrorists' claim amounts to that of being a state within the state. This is indeed what the Red Brigades in Italy wanted to have recognized when they kept politician Aldo Moro in a "people's prison," then "executed" him after "judgment."

8. Gaston Boissier's formulation in *La Fin du paganisme*, I, 57, (Paris, Hachette, 1891).

9. We recognize here the Socratic argument (earlier mentioned) but also the attitude of St. Paul, a Roman citizen, accepting Roman jurisdiction.

10. Christian B. Coleman, *Constantine the Great and Christianity*, p. 85, (New York, 1914, no publisher given).

11. It is false, according to Etienne Gilson, to identify the City of God with the Church and the City of This World with the state. The two are intermingled, according to St. Augustine. *Les Métamorphoses de la Cité de Dieu* (Paris: Lib. Phil. J. Vrin, 1952.

12. As Fustel de Coulanges argued in the *Ancient City* (*La Cité Antique*), ancient religion centered around the hearth and its gods. The "state religion" was an extended version of this piety.

13. *Politique tirée des propres paroles de l'Ecriture sainte*, III, 3,

IV, 70, (Librairie Droz, Genève, 1967). See also Jean Baechler, *Le pouvoir pur* (Paris: Calmann-Levy, 1978), where the author argues that, governing under the "grace of God," the kings implicitly recognized a higher authority, under which they stood.

14. *La naissance de l'esprit laïque,* in five volumes (Louvain/ Paris, Ed. E. Nauwelaerts, 1956).

15. G. Duby, *Le temps des cathédrales,* p. 266. It must be said (for more precision) that it was under the pontificate and powerful inspiration of Pope Gregory VII that the Church launched a great offensive against the worldly type religion, developed in the previous centuries. Gregory preached humility and Christian virtues, setting off evangelical movements of all sorts, out of which arose the mendicant orders but also the heretical sects. (Paris, Ed. Gallimard, 1976).

16. More correctly, religious basis, yes—insofar as it is derived from God, but not dependent on the papacy.

17. Some writers went so far as to suggest that the pope submit to the emperor, as Christ submitted to Pilate's judgment.

18. W. Ullmann, *Medieval Foundations of Renaissance Humanism* (Ithaca, N.Y.: Cornell University Press, 1977), p. 51.

19. *La naissance de l'esprit laïque,* III, 303, 381, (Louvain, Ed. Nauwelaerts, 1956).

20. *The Political Thought of William of Ockham,* p. 149, (Cambridge U. Press, 1974).

21. *Marsillius of Padua, the Defender of Peace,* (Columbia Univ. P., 1951, New York, 1956).

22. *Treatise on Law,* quest. 96, second article, (Chicago, Gateway, 1970).

23. Otto Gierke states that medieval political theories assumed that "never and nowhere can a purpose that is common to many be effectual unless the One rules over the Many, and directs the Many to the good" (*Political Theories of the Middle Ages,* p. 9), (Beacon Press, Boston, 1958).

24. There was hardly an opinion expressed in the Middle Ages, Gierke writes, that would free the sovereign, acting in the interest of the public weal, from the bonds of the moral law (op. cit., p. 86).

25. *Principles of Government and Politics in the Middle Ages,* pp. 223–24, (London, Methuen, 1961).

26. The Church, writes Gilson, does not engage in politics, but she cannot be indifferent to it. She has a direct religious authority over it, insofar as matters of faith and morals are inseparable from politics.

Chapter 2

1. For representatives of this view, see Fr. Robert Lenoble, *Histoire de l'idée de nature* (Paris, Albin Michel, 1969) and Thomas S. Kuhn, *The Structure of Scientific Revolutions* (1962), (Univ. of Chicago Press).

2. *What Is Political Philosophy?* p. 41, (Free Press, Glencoe, Ill., 1959).

3. It is this situation which requires the writing of this book.

4. *Natural Law and the Theory of Society,* p. 50, (Boston, Beacon Press, 1960).

5. Op. cit., p. 39.

6. Op. cit., p. 165.

7. *Of Human Nature,* p. 16, (French transl., Paris, Libr. Philosophique J. Vrin, 1971).

8. Ibid., p. 66.

9. George H. Sabine, *A History of Political Theory* (1973), p. 403.

10. Justus Möser remarked at the time, about Frederick the Great's Prussia, that the new philosophical theories consider the obstacles brought forth by historical developments as so many irritants that these theories must brutally eliminate.

11. G. P. Gooch and Harold Laski, *English Democratic Ideas in the Seventeenth Century,* p. 302, (Cambridge U. Press, 1954).

12. As an illustration of what has become of language, here is a sentence from the inaugural lecture at the Collège de France by literary critic Roland Barthes: "Language is fascistic because the sentences are based on subordination: subject, predicate, direct and indirect object," etc.

13. *Emile,* a profession of faith.

14. Jacques Droz, *Romantisme politique en Allemagne,* p. 12, (Paris, Armand Colin, 1963).

15. See the well-documented study by Ernst Benz, *Les sources mystiques de la philosophie romantique allemande* (Paris: J. Vrin, 1968).

16. *Discourses to the German Nation* (1807).

17. It should be noted that while Fichte was the initiator, and also the ideologue of the national creed as a historical force, a number of important thinkers became better and more prudent representatives of the German national ideology: Adam Müller, C. von Savigny, and later F. Tönnies.

18. There is today a revival of Maistrean studies in his native Savoie and elsewhere.

19. *Les Soirées de Saint-Petersbourg,* "Second Conversation," Paris, Lib. Garnier, no date given).

20. Op. Cit., "First Conversation."

21. Yet this general freedom creates a culture which ultimately turns against freedom and its liberal roots. See Daniel Bell, *The Cultural Contradictions of Capitalism* (New York: Basic Books, 1976).

22. It may be argued, of course, that it was the other way around—capitalism clearing the way for liberalism. This is the thesis that the Marxist would uphold. It comes down to the question: Which of the two (or more?) precedes: the movement of ideas or that of the merchandise?

23. *Spirit of the Laws,* book VIII, chapter 2. Two hundred years later, Walter Lippmann repeated Montesquieu's diagnosis, stating that the outcome of a liberal regime is the loss of power by the people who handed it to their manipulators, then to an elite corps "masked off from the mass of the people by special training and by special vows" (*The Public Philosophy,* p. 59).

24. Montesquieu, op. cit., book XI, chapter 6.

25. *The Public Philosophy,* p. 113, (Boston, Little, Brown, 1955).

26. H. Rommen, *The State in Catholic Thought,* p. 39, (New York, Greenwood Press, 1969).

27. The Catholic position is also accused of hypocrisy because

it is compatible with the legalization of prostitution, although not with the legalization of drug addiction and abortion. Let us remember St. Thomas's statement that the state should not pass laws for the enforcement of virtue, which implies as a corollary that its laws should not encourage vice. Prostitution, however, is a venial sin, nor is it encouraged, but only tolerated, thus falling into the category of custom, not law.

28. *The Church and the Liberal Society* (Princeton, N.J.: Princeton University Press, 1944), pp. 234-35.

29. *The State in Catholic Thought*, p. 68.

30. See my book *Christian Humanism*, chapters 1 and 2 (Chicago: Franciscan Herald Press, 1978).

31. V. A. Demant, *Religion and the Decline of Capitalism*, p. 113, (London, Faber and Faber, 1952).

32. *The State in Catholic Thought*, p. 343.

33. *Freedom in the Modern World*, p. 40, (London, Sheed & Ward, 1935).

34. Eric Weil, *Hegel et l'Etat*, p. 50, (Paris, Lib. Philos. Vrin, 1974).

35. The famous Hegelian dictum, "What is rational is real, what is real is rational."

36. On all this, see my book *God and the Knowledge of Reality*, part 2 (New York: Basic Books, 1973).

37. In Stalin's letter on the linguistic question, quoted in Gustave Wetter, *Le materialisme dialectique*, pp. 232, 345, 348, (Paris, Desclée De Brouwer, 1962).

38. In a book published in 1927, the Italian liberal historian, Guido de Ruggiero, wrote that although, according to liberalism, man needs no intermediary but only his own, unaided efforts to realize all the values of spiritual life, liberalism has now reconciled itself with the idea that "the State, the organ of coercion par excellence, has become the highest expression of liberty; the traditional enemy of the individual has reconstructed itself after the pattern of individual consciousness" (*The History of European Liberalism*, p. 353), (Boston, Beacon Hill, 1959).

39. *Introduction à la lecture de Hegel* (Paris, Gallimard, 1947).

40. Quoted from a debate, "Tyranny and the Philosopher," between A. Kojève and Leo Strauss.

41. *Tractatus theologico-politicus,* (Paris, Garnier, 1965).

42. Giuseppe Battisti, "Democracy in Spinoza's Unfinished *Tractatus Politicus,*" *Journal of the History of Ideas,* 38 (October/December 1977), 4.

Chapter 3

1. This is how St. Thomas argues for the person as a primary agent and for the state as a secondary agent: Civil society and its culmination, the state, constitute a *unity of order,* since they consist of many people; the individual person constitutes a *unity of substance.* The state is a human artifact, man is a being (*Commentary on Nichomachean Ethics,* I, 1).

2. Not all Gnostics were Christian, but the Gnostic movement, with its beginnings in Iran and the Near East, adopted views from the Old and New Testaments and became indistinguishable from other Christian heresies.

3. *Moral Man and Immoral Society,* p. 20, (Scribner, N.Y., 1932).

4. *Lettre aux dirigeants de l'Union Soviétique* (September 1973, Ed. du Seuil, Paris).

5. *Théologie de l'histoire,* p. 79, (Paris, Ed. du Seuil, 1968).

6. *Theology of Work,* pp. 45, 70, (Chicago, Reguery, 1966).

7. (Paris: Ed. La Cité Catholique, 1956). The original was published in Buenos Aires in 1945.

8. P. 168.

9. Some authors of this trend are Sigmund Freud, Herbert Marcuse, and Th. Roszak.

10. Quoted in I. W. Allen, *A History of Political Thought in the Sixteenth Century,* p. 96, (London, Methuen, 1960).

11. Luther's political involvement is another story. Aware that the cause of the Reformation depended on the good will of the German princes, such as the elector of Saxony, he became their partisan, first in crushing the peasant uprisings (around 1525), then in resisting the emperor (1530–40).

12. Such a statement usually enhances an author's reputation for "detached wisdom." Actually, it is the opposite of wisdom because it assumes that men are not rational and that their indi-

viduality is too precious to concern itself with a reasonable political arrangement.

13. *Church Dogmatics* and *The Word of God and the Word of Man*, (Harper, Torch Book, 1957).

14. *The Christian Community in the Midst of Political Change.*

15. *Christian Community and Civil Community*, p. 173, (In *Community, State and Church*, N.Y., Anchor Books, 1960).

16. Yet not for just any "theocracy." In *A Letter to American Christians* he wrote that the war against Hitler was beneficent and merciful and in the truest interest of even those who were not directly affected. "It is necessary, *now, now, now* [his emphasis] to act, help, fight with might and main."

17. *Natural Law*, p. 61, (N.Y., Sheed & Ward, 1965).

18. *What Is Political Philosophy?*, p. 223, (Free Press, Glencoe, Ill., 1959).

19. *The State in Catholic Thought*, p. 343. Jacques Droz, (Paris, A. Colin, 1963).

20. Quoted in *Le Romantisme politique en Allemagne* (1963), p. 84. Adam Müller was sharply critical of Adam Smith and his followers for being inconsequential: while their liberalism extended the influence of Enlightenment philosophy, they elaborated a political economy which, in its narrowness, dealt only with material interests, figures, and needs.

21. *Community and Society*, p. 82, (Michigan State Univ. Press, 1957).

22. *Natural Law*, p. 86.

23. *The State in Catholic Thought*, pp. 41–42.

24. *Discourses*, III, 1.

25. *The News World*, Aug. 13, 1978.

26. From *The Remnant*, July 19, 1978.

27. Reading these documents provokes never ending marvel at their timeless wisdom. In the mid-thirteenth century, Innocent IV upheld the right of conquered Moslems to property and the legitimacy of non-Christian rulers; in 1537, Paul III declared the Amerindians' right to property and freedom, even if they were not converted; in 1639, Urban VIII decreed excommunication for those who deprived the Amerindians of their liberty

or property. The Church, according to its enemies, always rules in favor of the powerful but these instances show that it ruled against the powerful, in favor of justice.

Chapter 4

1. This is the title of the book (New York: Sheed and Ward, 1960).

2. The first chapter in part 1 of John Courtney Murray's book bears the title "E Pluribus Unum: The American Consensus." "Consensus" and "unity" figure in the title of three other chapters of part 1.

3. Published by the National Committee of Catholic Laymen (New York, 1978), 46 pages.

4. Hitchcock's subthesis is that Kennedy renounced his Catholic principles, as no Protestant president has ever done and no Jewish president would ever do. Thus he served as a model for other liquidators of Catholic principles, whether bishops, Catholic writers, or priest-congressmen.

5. For example, in *Christian Humanism: A Critique of the Secular City and Its Ideology* (Chicago: Franciscan Herald Press, 1978).

6. *An Essay on the Development of Christian Doctrine* (1878), (Image Books, Doubleday, 1960).

7. *Osservatore Romano*, Dec. 12, 1976.

8. The founder of the Paulist order, Fr. Isaac Hecker, celebrated the new tolerance represented by America, where society in a way embodied the Christian ideal.

9. Tocqueville saw in it the promise that the Church might remain an independent, and partly uninvolved, influence in a democratic regime. Due to this presence and influence, democracy might be saved from its self-destructive and corrupting inclinations. Without the assumption of such a durable influence by the Church, Tocqueville was very pessimistic about democratic regimes' serving their citizens.

10. *The First Amendment and the Future of American Democracy* (New York: Basic Books, 1976).

11. *Essays on the Scientific Study of Politics.*

12. For the Mexican bishop, socialism is the only solution for Latin America's poor. He finds in Castro's Cuba a model society, and believes that the Church's "new discourse" must be based on Marx, as the old discourse was based on Aristotle. Mendez Arceo proudly underlines the fact that he wears neither the pectoral cross nor the bishop's ring.

13. In the diocesan paper *Eglise de Grenoble,* Matagrin writes that while the Church has no social model or political program to offer, it takes cognizance of the failure of liberalism to achieve a consensus, as well as the breakup of Marxism into conflicting currents. At the same time, the French bishop notes that socialism is becoming democratic and that this represents a positive promise for the future.

14. The closest comparison is with the "Voltairean" abbés of the eighteenth and nineteenth centuries. Mocking Christian truths and forms of belief, they were enamored with the *douceur de vivre* in the salons, other mundane gatherings, and philosophical cliques, where atheism or deism was adhered to as the only tolerable form of thought for "enlightened" people.

15. A typically malicious but not rare illustration of the subservience of the Church to the state was recently given by moral theologian Bernard Quelquejeu (in France) concerning abortion. It is legitimate for Christians, writes Fr. Quelquejeu, to reject abortion for themselves, but they should not impose their point of view on others, since Vatican II recognized the temporal autonomy of the state. Christian moral law, linked to Christian faith, should not impose itself on law that is promulgated by the state. (In the same way, then, Christians should not oppose or obstruct state law when it legalizes genocide?)

16. Commenting on the medieval Church, Walter Ullmann writes that "papal government was so efficient because the ancient, Ciceronian precept that law, in order to be effective, must have the consent of those to whom it applies, found a concrete application: faith replaced the Ciceronian consent." (*Principles of Government and Politics in the Middle Ages,* Methuen & Co., London, 1961, P. 95).—The institutional strength of the Church is underlined by Joseph R. Strayer: "on many points

already the tenth century Church possessed the attributes of a State (for example, durable institutions) and was to acquire more such attributes, such as papal sovereignty." (*Les origines medievales de l'Etat moderne*, Paris, Payot, 1979.)

17. "Vocation consists in the preaching of the Word and the illumination of the Holy Spirit. . . . The certainty of our vocation grants us the certainty of our election. Those who stumble never had the true faith because vocation can never be lost." (Calvin, *Institutions*, Book III.). Also: "I say that the reprobates never reach the revelation (of the true faith), the revelation of the certitude to possess the true faith, the secret revelation of their salvation, because Scripture grants it to the faithful alone." (Quoted by Fr. Ch. Boyer, S. J., *Calvin et Luther, Accords et Differences*, Ed. Univ. Greg., Rome, 1973, p. 72). And more drastically: "If you entertain some doubts about my calling, it is enough for me that it is quite clear to my own satisfaction." (Calvin to a Genevan burgher, in 1538, in Michael Walzer: *The Revolution of the Saints, A study in the origins of radical politics*, Harvard Univ. Press, 1965.